Downton Lace

BERTHA KEMP

Downton Lace

Dryad Press Ltd, London

ACKNOWLEDGEMENT

The Publisher and Author wish to acknowledge the help
given by Edna Sutton and Mary Moseley in the
preparation of this book.

Kemp, Bertha
Downton lace.
1. Bobbin lace. Making-Manuals
I. Title
746.2′22

ISBN 0-85219-745-4

Typeset by Latimer Trend & Company Ltd, Plymouth
and printed in Great Britain by
Anchor Brendon Ltd.
Tiptree, Essex.

for the publishers
Dryad Press Ltd
8 Cavendish Square
London W1M 0AJ

CONTENTS

INTRODUCTION 7
  Making Downton Lace 7
  Stitches used in Downton Lace 8
  Half Stitch 8
  Cloth Stitch 8
  Honeycomb Stitch 9
  Purl pin 9
  The Foot 10
  Catchpin 10
  Ground stitch 10

GROUP ONE: **Introductory** 11
  Pattern 126 12
  Egg and Rasher 14
  Pattern 165 16
  The Earring (Pattern 140) 18
  The Double Brick (Pattern 15) 20
  Church Windows (Pattern 21) 22
  Duke's Garter (Pattern 108) 24
  The Bean 25

GROUP TWO: **Intermediate** 27
  Pattern 52 28
  The Iron 29
  The Ace of Diamonds 31
  Pattern 186 32
  Pattern 67 34
  Pattern 53 36
  Cheese Cutter 37
  Ace of Clubs 39

GROUP THREE: **Advanced** 42
  Pattern 139 43
  Pattern 176 45
  Pattern 181 46
  The Arches 49
  The Oak Leaf 51
  Roll and Pat of Butter 53
  The Strawberry 54
  The Grecian 57
  Pattern 59 60

SUPPLIERS 62
FURTHER READING 63
INDEX 64

INTRODUCTION

It is not known exactly when lace was first made in Downton. Daniel Defoe, author of Robinson Crusoe, said that in 1731 beautiful lace was made in Blandford, which is not far from Downton, so maybe that was when lace first arrived there. It was while I was attending Minstead school, in 1917, that Miss Geraldine Jefferys called to enquire whether any of the girls would like to attend the village hall on Saturdays for lessons in lacemaking.

Many attended these lessons, but as far as I know I am now the only person from these classes still making lace. The same thing happened with lacemaking classes in other villages, including Calmore. The lacemaking classes were eventually wound up in 1925 because the girls were old enough to go to work. They no longer had any time to make lace.

The old Downton lace industry has made wedding gifts for the Royal Family since 1922, when I made pieces for HRH Princess Mary. Since then, I have made gifts for HRH Princess Anne and Captain Mark Phillips, Prince Charles and Princess Diana, and Prince Andrew and Miss Sarah Ferguson, on the occasions of their marriages. Downton lace is made on a bolster-shaped pillow packed tightly with barley straw. The patterns have names such as *Egg and Rasher, Egg and Drop, The Arches, The Garland*, and the *Downton Daisy* (a troublesome pattern to work). These names are only a few of the two hundred Downton patterns. The Downton lace industry finally ended in 1965. All money, master prickings, books, etc., were given to the Salisbury Museum. These items, together with gifts already made by Miss Geral-

dine Jeffreys and Miss Glyn, were donated to the Museum to form a valuable addition to the record of the history of Wiltshire.

Abbreviations used in this book

RH	Right hand
LH	Left hand
cp	Catch pin
h st	Half stitch
cl st	Cloth stitch
hc st	Honeycomb stitch
PP	Purl pin
ft	Foot
gr st	Ground stitch
tw	Twist

Making Downton lace

Prick out the design so that the length will fit round the bolster. Take care to match the lengths of pattern. Pin carefully to the pillow, matching the last join. In this way one can work a desired length of lace without removing the pins and moving the lace. Several threads may be knotted together, hung on a pin at the back of the pricking; with your right hand make another loop about the pin and pull firmly. Several pins may be located and used in this manner. Each pricking is started with the footing on the left-hand side, the net, followed by the heading. Place the pins in a slightly backwards direction. The old Downton prickings are numbered 1 to 200 as well as having individual names.

Stitches used in Downton lace

Half stitch (h st)

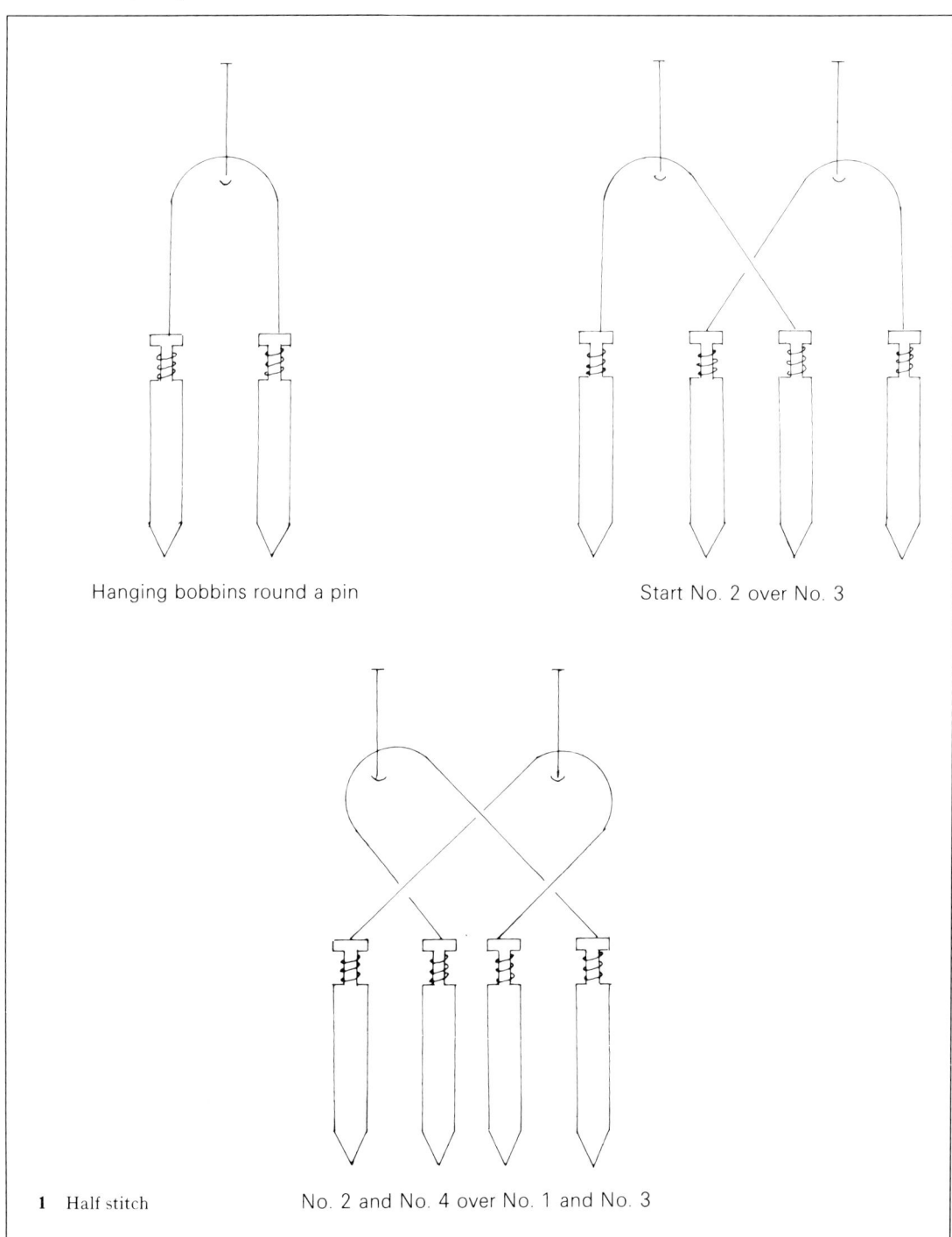

Hanging bobbins round a pin

Start No. 2 over No. 3

1 Half stitch

No. 2 and No. 4 over No. 1 and No. 3

Cloth stitch (cl st)

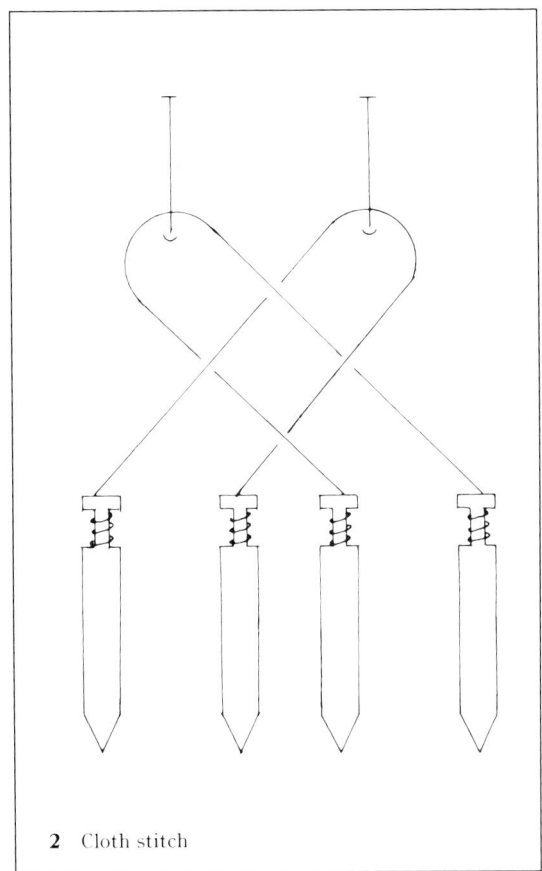

2 Cloth stitch

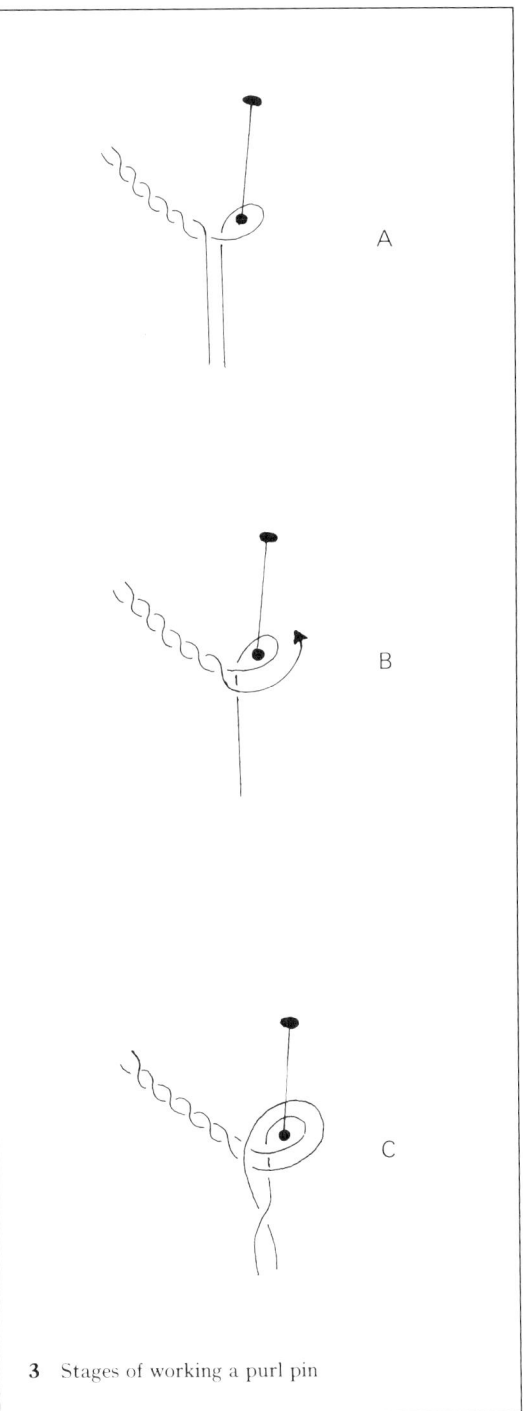

3 Stages of working a purl pin

Honeycomb stitch (hc st)

H st, twist each pair once. Pin. Close the pin with the same stitch.

Purl Pin (PP)

Work a cl st, and twist the workers seven times. Twist the pin over and under the right-hand thread. Place the pin into the pin hole. Twist the LH thread about this pin in an anti-clockwise direction. Firm the threads carefully, twist twice, work a cl st with the passive pair. Twist each pair once.

The foot (ft)

Counting from the left, select the fourth pair. Work two cl sts to the left. Twist the worker pair twice and support this pair about a pin at No. 1. Work a cl st with the first pair. Twist each pair twice, cl st through two pairs to the right.

Catch pin (cp)

Twist the worker pair three times, support it on a pin at No. 2. With the next pair on the right work a h st and two twists on each pair. Use the RH pair as the next worker.

Ground stitch (gr st)

H st, two twists. Pin between the pairs.

Downton whole stitch

Downton whole stitch is a skill used in Downton Lace. In order to avoid confusion with whole stitch (as we know it today), the Downton whole stitch will be referred to throughout this book as a cloth stitch and twist on both pairs of bobbins.

GROUP ONE:

Introductory

All patterns use 120 cotton thread and No. 12 DMC Coton Perle for the gimp unless otherwise stated.

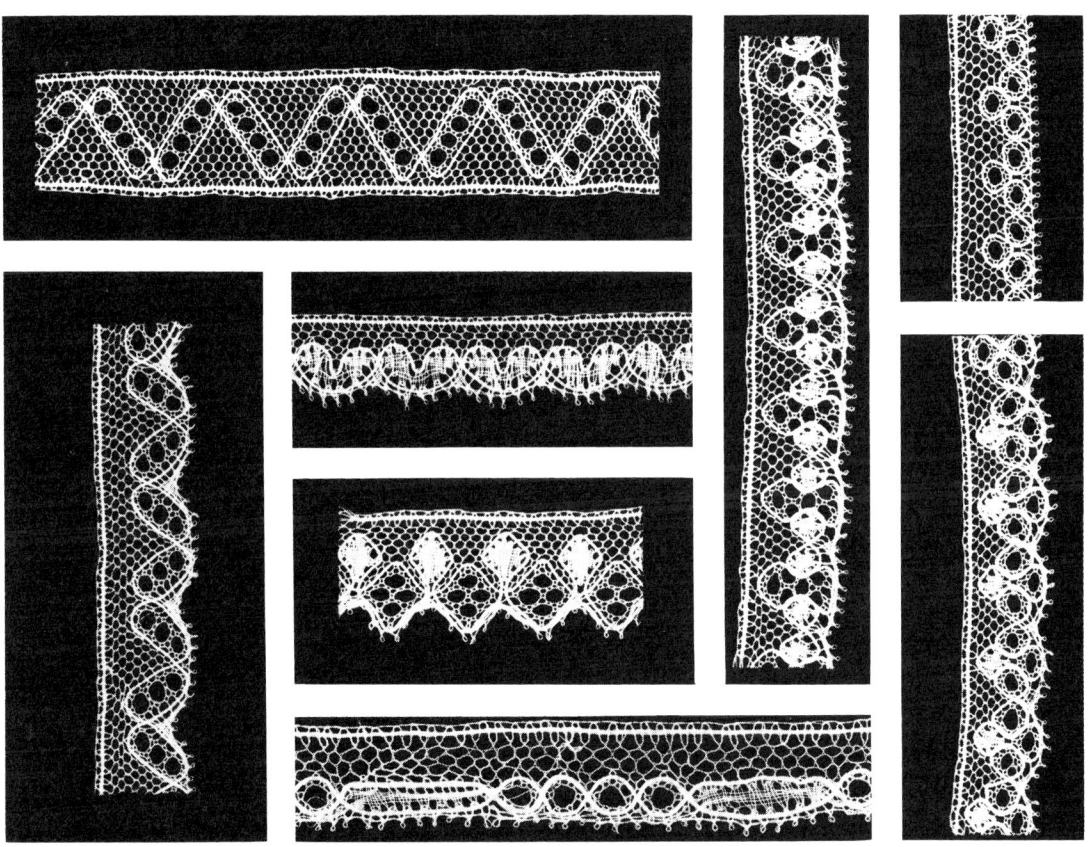

Pattern 126

The first lesson in Downton lace is worked with 120 cotton thread, 28 bobbins and No. 12 DMC Coton Perle, 2 gimp threads. This lesson will explain the setting up, the footing, the catch pin (cp) working the ground stitch (gr st) and the honeycomb stitch (hc st) used in working the 'eggs', and later used as a ground stitch. These stitches are some of the techniques used in Downton lace.

4 Pricking for Pattern 126

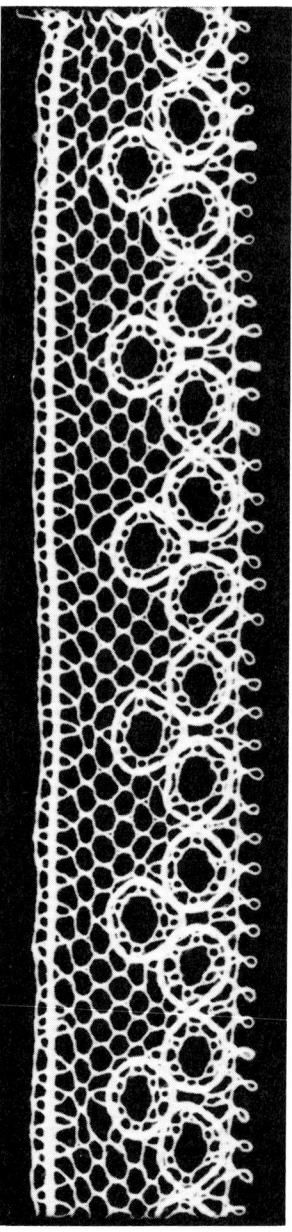

6 Pattern 126, introducing 'eggs' and a reverse catch pin

5 Technical drawing for Pattern 126

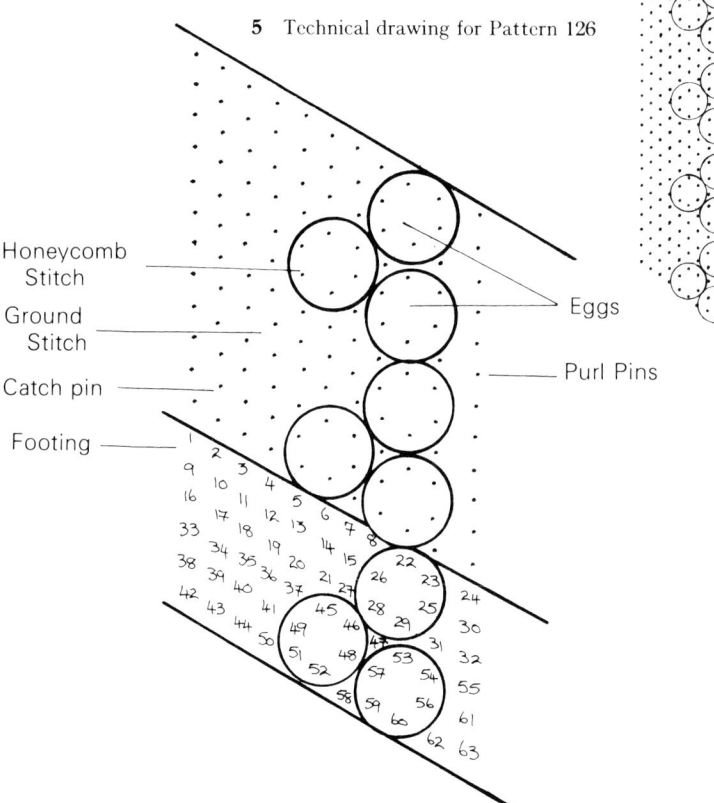

Honeycomb Stitch

Ground Stitch

Catch pin

Footing

Eggs

Purl Pins

Divide the threads into four groups. Knot each group and put a pin through each knot. Place the pins at the top of the pricking ready to set up. Hang the gimp threads on a pin and place into position ready for working.

Setting up
a) Start with the ft, at the LH side, by working pin 1, and the cp at 2 (Fig. 5). Work pins 3, 4, 5, 6, 7 and 8 in gr st (Fig. 5).
b) Work the ft at pin 9, the cp at pin 10 and the gr st at 11, 12, 13, 14 and 15.
c) Work the ft at pin 16, the cp at pin 17, and the gr st at 18, 19, 20 and 21.

The first egg
a) Pass the LH gimp through two pairs, and the RH gimp through two pairs.
b) Using the two centre pairs, work a hc st (Fig. 5), and close the pin at pin 22. With the RH centre pair and the pair on the right, work the same stitch at pin 23.
c) Pass the RH gimp through one pair to the left and work the PP at 24, Fig. 5. Pass the RH gimp through one pair to the right. Work a hc st and close the pin at pin 25.
d) Using the top LH centre pair and the pair on the left, work a hc st and close the pin at pin 26. Now pass the LH gimp through one pair to the right, work a gr st and put up the pin to the right of the threads at pin 27. This is now termed 'a reverse cp'.
e) Pass the LH gimp through one pair to the left, work a hc st, pin and close at pin 28. With the two centre pairs work a hc st and close at pin 29. Pass the LH gimp through two pairs to the right and the RH gimp through two pairs to the left. Cross the gimps left over right. Work the PP at pin 30.
f) Work a hc st and close at pin 31 and work the PP at pin 32.
g) Return to the ft edge and work pin 33 and the cp at 34. Now work the gr st at pins 35, 36 and 37. Work the ft at pin 38, the cp at pin 39 and the gr st at pins 40 and 41. Work the ft

at pin 42, the cp at pin 43 and the gr st at pin 44.

The second egg
a) Pass the LH gimp through five pairs to the left. With the centre pairs work a hc st, pin and close at pin 45.
b) With the RH centre pair and the pair on the right, work a hc st, pin and close at pin 46. Pass the RH gimp through one pair to the left. Work another hc st, pin and close at pin 47. Pass the RH gimp through one pair to the right. Work hc st. Pin and close at pin 48.
c) With the LH centre pair and the pair on the left, work a hc st, pin and close at pin 49.
d) Pass the LH gimp through one pair to the right. Work a reverse cp at pin 50. Pass the LH gimp through one pair to the left. Work a hc st, pin and close at pin 51.
e) Work a hc st, pin and close at pin 52. Pass the LH gimp through five pairs to the right. Cross the gimps, left over right.
f) Pass the RH gimp through two pairs and the LH gimp through two pairs.

The third egg
a) Using the two centre pairs work a hc st, pin and close at pin 53. With the RH centre pair and one from the right work a hc st, pin and close at pin 54. Pass the RH gimp through one pair to the left and work PP at pin 55.
b) Pass the RH gimp through one pair to the right and work a hc st, pin and close at pin 56. With the LH centre pair and the pair on the left work a hc st, pin and close at pin 57.
c) Pass the LH gimp through one pair to the right. Work a reverse cp at pin 58. Pass the LH gimp through one pair to the left. Work a hc st, pin and close at pin 59.
d) With the centre pairs work a hc st, pin and close at pin 60. Pass the LH gimp through two pairs and the RH gimp through two pairs. Cross the gimps.
e) Work the PP at pin 61. Hc st, pin and close at pin 62. Work the PP at pin 63.

These instructions complete the first lesson and one heading of the pattern.

Egg and Rasher

The second lesson, a traditional edging, is worked with 120 cotton, 26 bobbins and No. 12 DMC Coton Perle, 2 gimps. If you look at the photograph (Fig. 8) you will see a rasher of bacon and four eggs.

Setting up
Prepare the threads as described on p. 13 and place them into position. Hang the pair of gimps from a pin.

The rasher
a) Start with the ft at the left hand side. Work the ft at pin 1, and the cp at pin 2. Gr st are worked at pins 3, 4, 5 and 6.
b) Return to the footing and work the ft at pin 7, the cp at pin 8 and the gr st at pins 9, 10 and 11. Work the ft at pin 12, the cp at pin 13 and the gr st at pins 14 and 15.
c) Pass the LH gimp through two pairs to the left. Pass the RH gimp through two pairs to the right. Using the two centre pairs cl st pin and close at pin 16. Cl st to the left and pass the gimp to the right. Work a reverse catch pin at pin 17. Pass the LH gimp back to the left. Cl st to the right and close the pin at pin 18. Pass the RH gimp through one pair to the left and work PP19. Pass the RH gimp back and leave.
d) Using the worker pair from pin 18, Cl st to the left. Pass the LH gimp through one pair to the right and leave. Work the gr st at pin 21 and the reverse catch pin at pin 22.
e) Pass the LH gimp through one pair to the left. Cl st to the right. Pin and close at pin 20. Pass the RH gimp to the left. Work PP 23. Pass the gimp back and leave. Make sure you have made the correct number of twists before and after passing the gimp.
f) Using the worker from pin 20, cl st to the left. Leave this worker pair. Work pins 25–29. Pass the LH gimp to the right.
g) Work the reverse catch pin at pin 30. Pass the LH gimp to the left. Cl st to the right and close at pin 24. Using the RH pair from pin 24, pass the RH gimp to the left and work the PP at pin 31. Pass the RH gimp to the right and leave.
h) Work pins 33–37. Take the worker from pin 24. Cl st to the left, and pass the gimp through the worker pair. Work the reverse catch pin at pin 38. (Three twists on the LH pair and one on the RH pair.)
i) Pass the LH gimp back and cl st to the right. Pin and close at pin 32. Pass the RH gimp to the left and work the PP at pin 39. Pass the RH gimp back and leave.
j) Work pins 41–45. Using the LH pair from pin 32, cl st to the left. Pass the LH gimp to the right. Work the reverse catch pin at pin 46. Pass the LH gimp to the left and cl st to the right. Pin and close at pin 40.
k) Pass the RH gimp to the left and work PP 47. Pass the gimp back and leave. Work pins 49–53.
l) Using the LH pair from pin 40, cl st to the left. Pass the LH gimp to the right, and work the reverse catch pin at pin 54. Continue in this way until pin 71 is reached. Close the centre pin at pin 71.
m) Pass the LH gimp through two pairs to the right. Pass the RH gimp through two pairs to the left. Cross the gimps, left over right. With the pair from pin 64 work the PP at pin 72. Work pin 73a with the RH pair from pin 71 and the pair from pin 72 (h st 1 tw, pin and close). Work the PP at pin 73.
n) Work pins 74–79, pins 80–84, and pins 85–88. Pass the LH gimp through two pairs and the RH gimp through two pairs.
o) The four eggs are worked in the same way as those in the first lesson. Follow the stages in numerical order, working the eggs and pin 98 in hc st. Take care to make the correct number of twists before and after passing the gimp threads. Pass the pairs, used to work the PP, back through the gimp thread.

These instructions complete the heading.

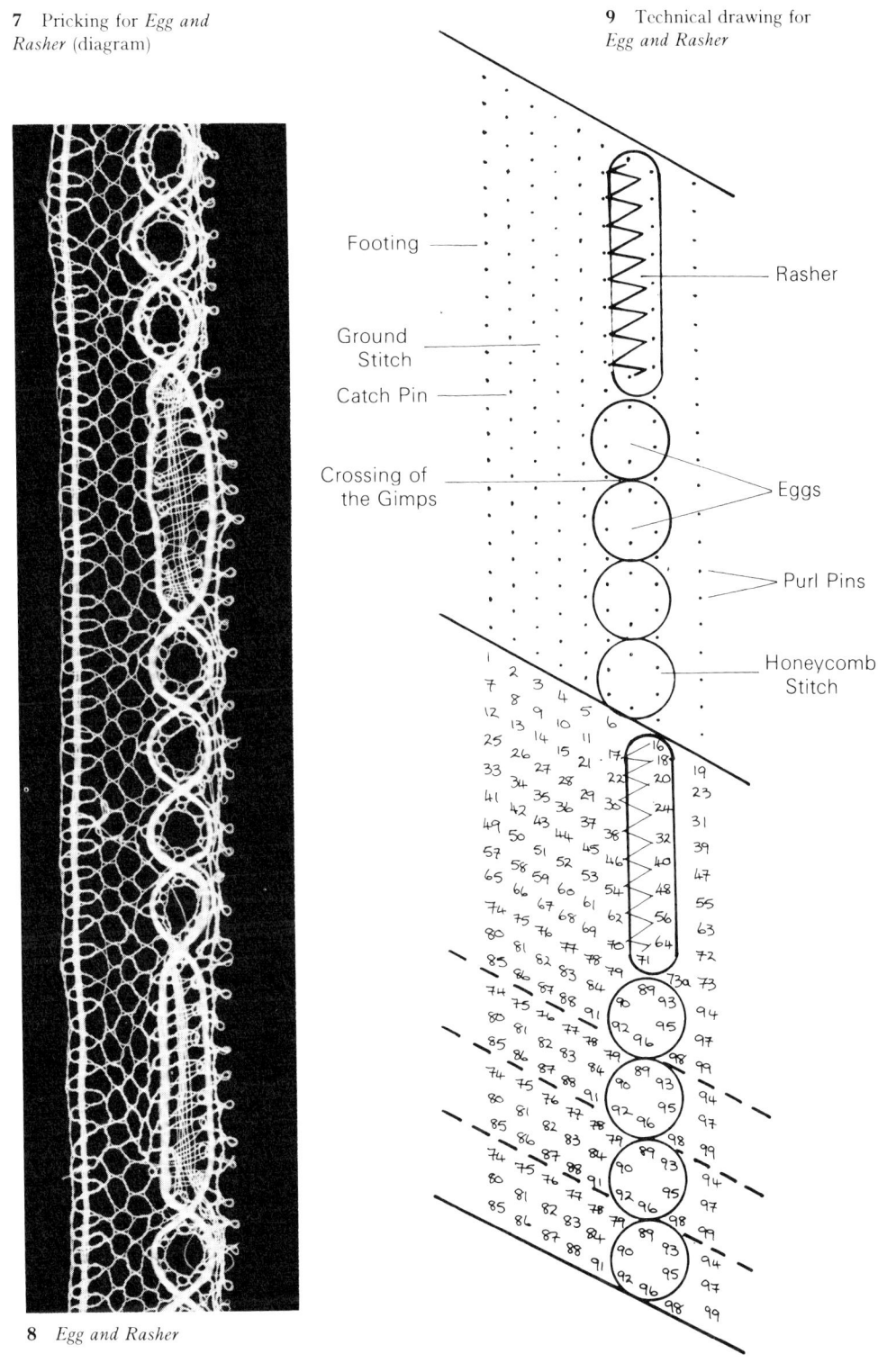

7 Pricking for *Egg and Rasher* (diagram)

8 *Egg and Rasher*

9 Technical drawing for *Egg and Rasher*

Footing

Ground Stitch

Catch Pin

Crossing of the Gimps

Rasher

Eggs

Purl Pins

Honeycomb Stitch

Pattern 165

The third lesson introduces one or two new features of Downton lace. This design needs **34** bobbins and **2** gimp bobbins, using the same threads as before. The main feature introduced here is the movement of the threads in the heading, the RH edge, to work the PP. Look at the photograph (Fig. 10) and you may notice a small area of cl st in the 'dip'. Prepare the threads as described on p. 13 and place them at the top of the pricking.

Setting up
a) Work the ft at pin 1 and the cp at pin 2. Work the gr st at pins 3–8. Return to the ft edge and work the ft at pin 9, the cp at pin 10 and the gr st at pins 11–15.
b) Work in numerical order until pin 35 has been worked.

The top cloth stitch drop
a) Pass the RH gimp to the right through three pairs, and the LH gimp through three pairs to the left. Twist each pair once.
b) With the two centre pairs work a cl st and close the pin at pin 36. Cl st to the right and close the pin at pin 37.
c) Complete the drop, closing the two centre pairs at pin 43. One pair must be thrown out at pins 39–42 and both pairs at pin 43. Make one twist on each pair.
d) Pass the LH gimp to the right through three pairs, and the RH gimp to the left through three pairs. Cross the gimps.
e) Pass the LH gimp to the left through seven pairs, and the RH gimp to the right through four pairs. Twist each pair twice ready to work the hc st.
f) Work the hc st at pin 44. Pass the RH gimp through one pair to the left and work the PP at pin 45. Cl st through the passive threads and pass the gimp back. Work a hc st at pin 46. Pass the RH gimp back and cl st through the passives and work the PP at pin 47.
g) Cl st back to the left and pass the gimp back

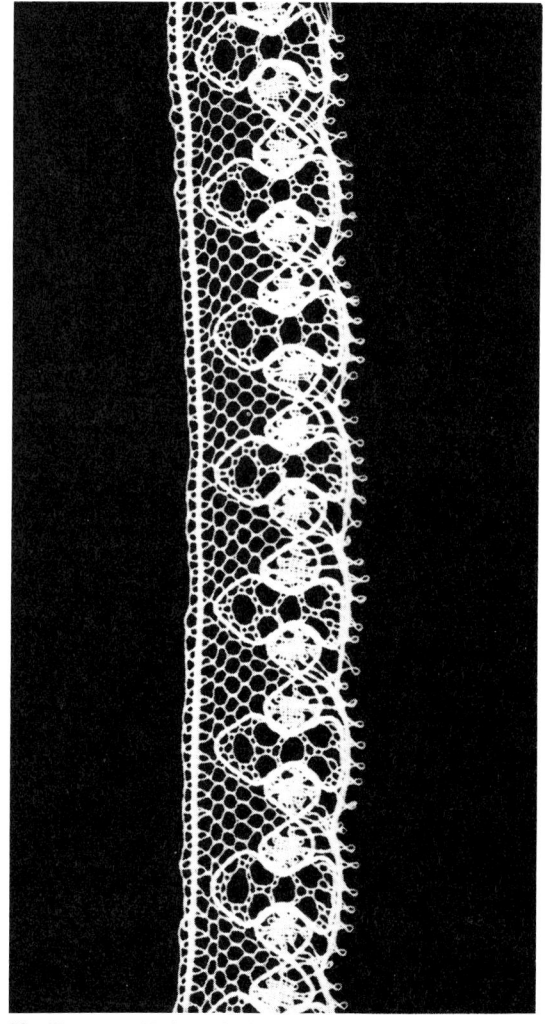

10 Pattern 165, introducing the 'diamond'

to the right. Work the hc st at pins 48, 49 and 50. Pass the gimp back, cl st through the passive threads and work the PP at pin 51. Pass the RH gimp back to the right.
h) Work the separates, hc st, at pins 52, 53, 54 and 55. Pass the RH gimp to the left, cl st through the passive threads and work the PP at pin 56. Pass the gimp back and work the hc st at pins 57, 58, 59 and 60.
i) Work the separates at pins 61 and 62. Work the hc st at pins 63, 64, 65 and 66. Pass the LH

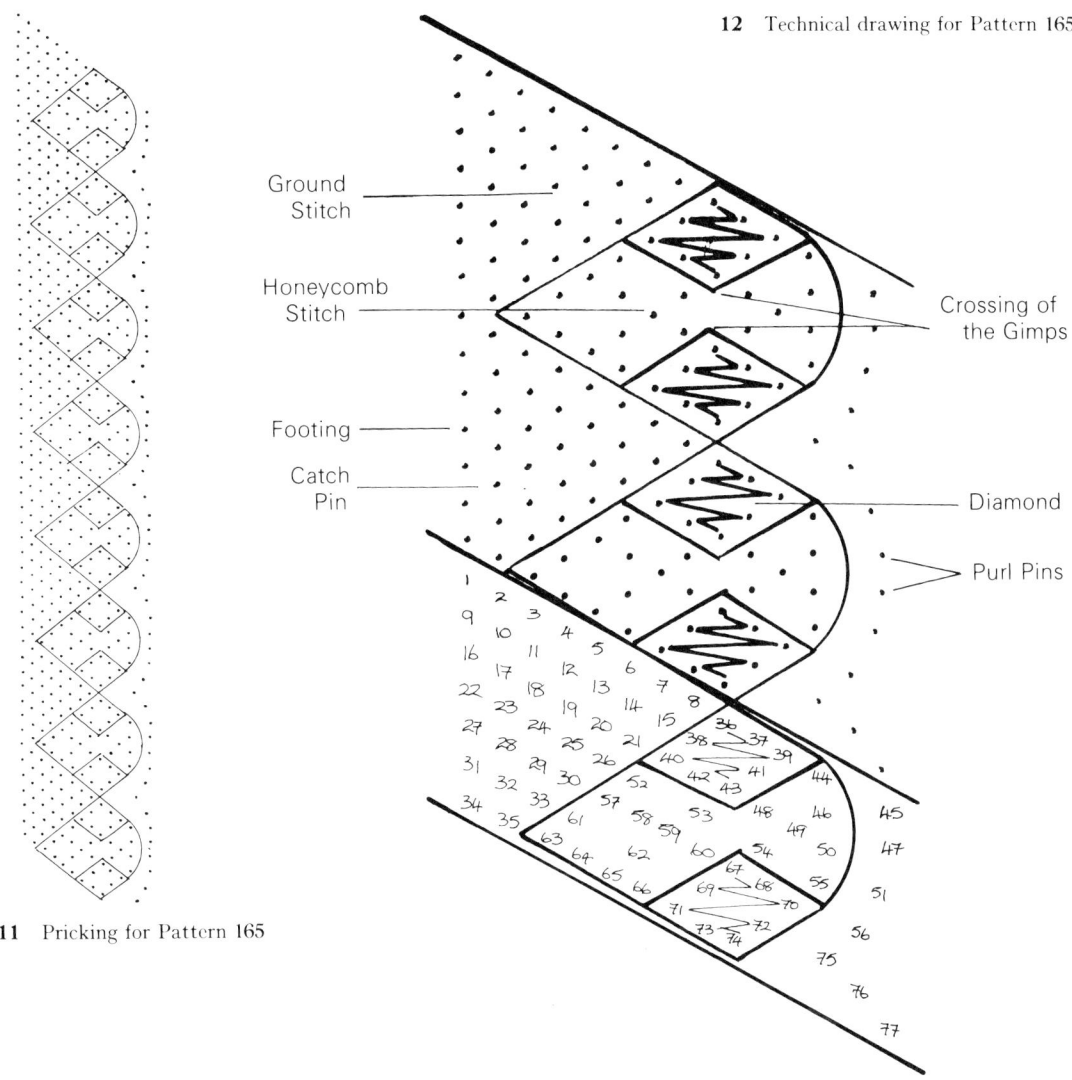

12 Technical drawing for Pattern 165

Ground Stitch

Honeycomb Stitch

Footing

Catch Pin

Crossing of the Gimps

Diamond

Purl Pins

11 Pricking for Pattern 165

gimp through seven pairs and the RH gimp through three pairs. Cross the gimps.

j) Pass the LH gimp to the left through three pairs, and the RH gimp to the right through three pairs. Make the appropriate twists on each pair.

The bottom cloth stitch drop

a) Using the two centre pairs, cl st and close the pin at pin **67**. Cl st to the right and close the pin at pin **68**. Complete the 'drop' working in numerical order, finally working the two centre pairs at pin **74** (see Fig. 12).

b) Pass the LH gimp to the right through three pairs, and the RH gimp to the left through three pairs. Cross the gimps.

c) Using the pair from pin **70** work the PP at pin **75**, using the pair from pin **72**, work PP **76**, using the pair from pin **74**, work the PP at pin **77**. Pass the pairs used to work the PP back through the gimp thread.

These instructions complete the heading.

The Earring

The fourth lesson provides more practice in working the Downton 'drops'. This design needs 32 bobbins and two gimp threads. The edge is curved, therefore there will be a small area of cl st in the 'dip' and care should be taken to work the picots with the correct pairs. Group the threads and the gimps and place at the top of the pricking ready to work.

Setting up
a) Start by working the ft at pin 1, the cp at pin 2, and the gr st at pins 3–7. Work in numerical order until pin 27 has been worked.

The first drop
a) Pass the LH gimp through three pairs to the right and the RH gimp through three pairs to the left.
b) Work the first drop in hc st, working the first stitch at pin 28. With the centre pair and the pair to the right work a hc st, pin and close at pin 29. Repeat at pin 30–34. Using the two centre pairs work pin 35.
b) Pass the LH gimp through three pairs. Pass the RH gimp through three pairs. Cross the gimp threads left over right.
c) Pass the LH gimp through six pairs to the left, and the RH gimp through three pairs. There are no twists between the gimp threads when two gimps are passed close together.
d) At pin 36 work a hc st, pin and close, repeat at pin 37. Pass the RH gimp to the left and work PP 38. Pass the gimp back to the right and work a hc st, pin and close at pin 39, pass the RH gimp to the left and work PP 40.
e) At the LH side of the drop, work pins 41, 42, 43 and the centre pin 44. Work PP 45. Pass the RH gimp through the pairs from pins 39, 44, 43 and 42. Cross the gimps. Put LH gimp through six pairs.

The cloth stitch drop
a) Make sure that the gimp has been passed through all the pairs needed to work the third LH drop. With the two centre pairs, cl st, pin and close at pin 46. Cl st to the right, pin and

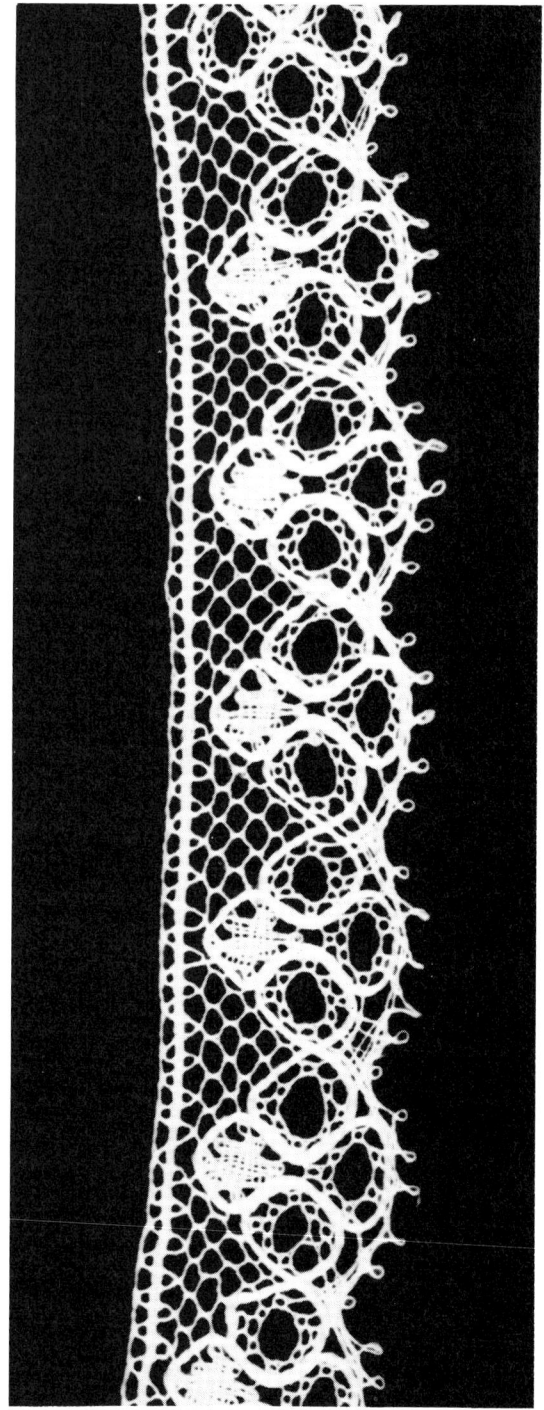

13 *The Earring*, introducing the 'drop'

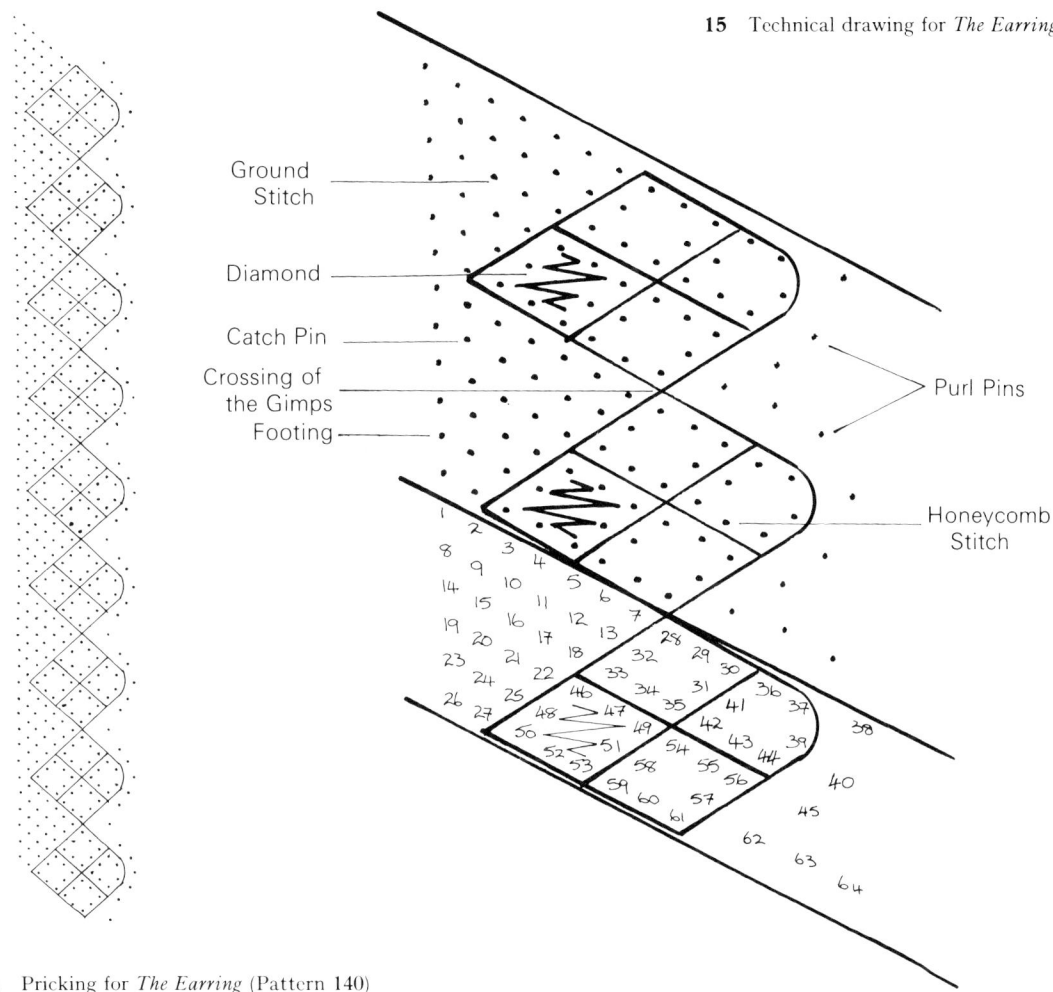

15 Technical drawing for *The Earring*

Ground Stitch

Diamond

Catch Pin

Crossing of the Gimps

Footing

Purl Pins

Honeycomb Stitch

14 Pricking for *The Earring* (Pattern 140)

close pin **47**. Work the pins in numerical order, finishing with the two centre pairs at pin **53**.
b) Make sure that one pair of bobbins has been thrown out at pins **49–52** and two pairs at pin **53**.
c) Pass the LH gimp through six pairs and cross the gimps. Pass the RH gimp through three pairs and the LH gimp through three pairs.

The third drop
a) Make sure that two twists have been made on all the pairs needed to work this drop. Using the two centre pairs work a hc st, pin and close at pin **54**.

b) Finish working the third drop, following the numerical system, finishing with centre pin, pin **61**.
c) Pass the LH gimp through three pairs to the right and the RH gimp through three pairs to the left.
d) Cross the gimps left over right.
e) Using the pair from pin **56**, work PP **62**. Using the pair from pin **57**, work PP **63**. Using the pair from pin **58**, work PP **64**.
f) Pass the RH gimp through these three pairs ready to work the next heading. Pass the pairs used to work the PP, back through the gimp thread.

These instructions complete the heading.

The Double Brick

The fifth lesson introduces an insertion to this group of lessons. The same threads are used as before, 40 bobbins and two gimp threads. Prepare the bobbins and the gimp threads as described on p. 13.

The first brick

a) Start at the ft, on the LH side, work the ft at pin 1, cp at pin 2 and gr st at pins 3 and 4.

b) Work the ft at pin 5, cp at pin 6, and gr st at pin 7. Work the ft at pin 8 and the cp at pin 9.

c) Pass the LH gimp to the left through three pairs, and the RH gimp to the right through nine pairs.

d) Work a hc st, pin and close at pin 10. Work to the right in numerical order (pins 11–19). Return to the left and work pin 20 and the separates 21, 22 and 23.

e) Work pins 24–32 in hc st. Make sure a pair of bobbins is thrown out from each pin, two from pin 32.

f) Pass the LH gimp to the right through nine pairs and the RH gimp to the left through three pairs. Cross the gimps.

g) Return to the footing and work in numerical order the ft, cp and gr st from pin 33 finishing with pin 86.

h) At the RH edge work the ft at pin 87, cp at 88 and the gr st at pins 89 and 90. Continue in this way until pin 95 is worked.

i) Pass the LH gimp to the left through nine pairs and the RH gimp to the right through three pairs.

The second brick

a) Start by working a hc st, with the centre pairs at pin 96. Continue working the brick in numerical order, finishing with pin 118. Cross the gimps.

b) Pass the LH gimp to the right through three pairs and the RH gimp to the left through nine pairs.

c) Start the ft at pin 119, cp at 120, working in numerical order finishing with pin 172.

This completes the instructions for the heading.

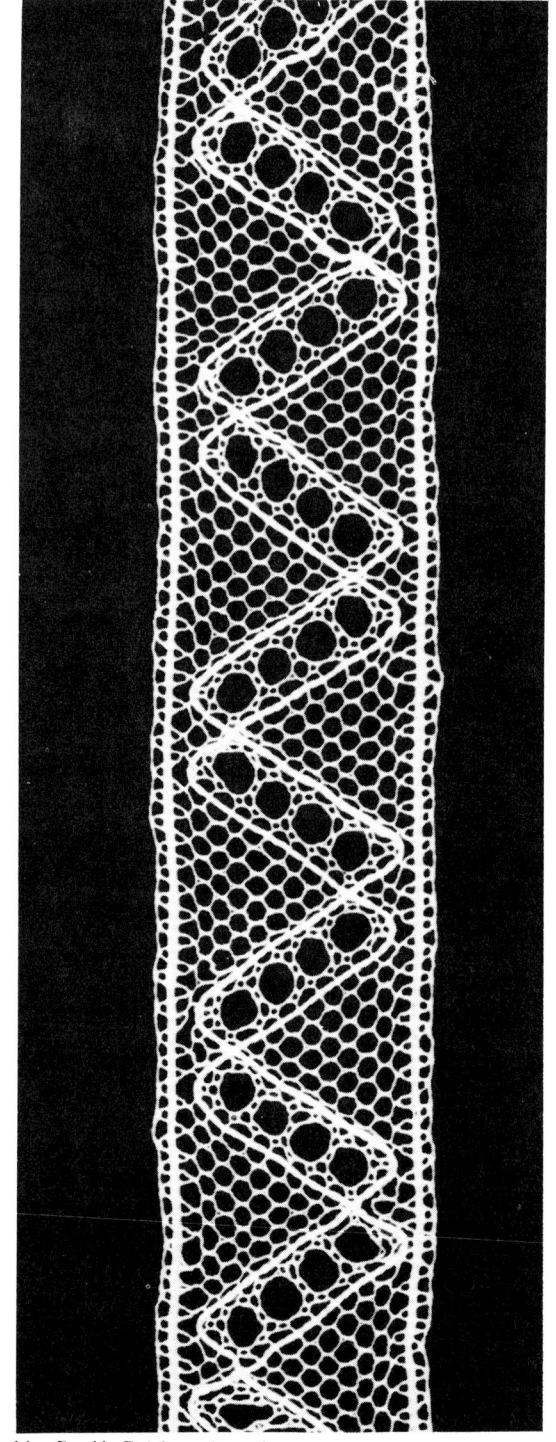

16 *Double Brick*, an insertion

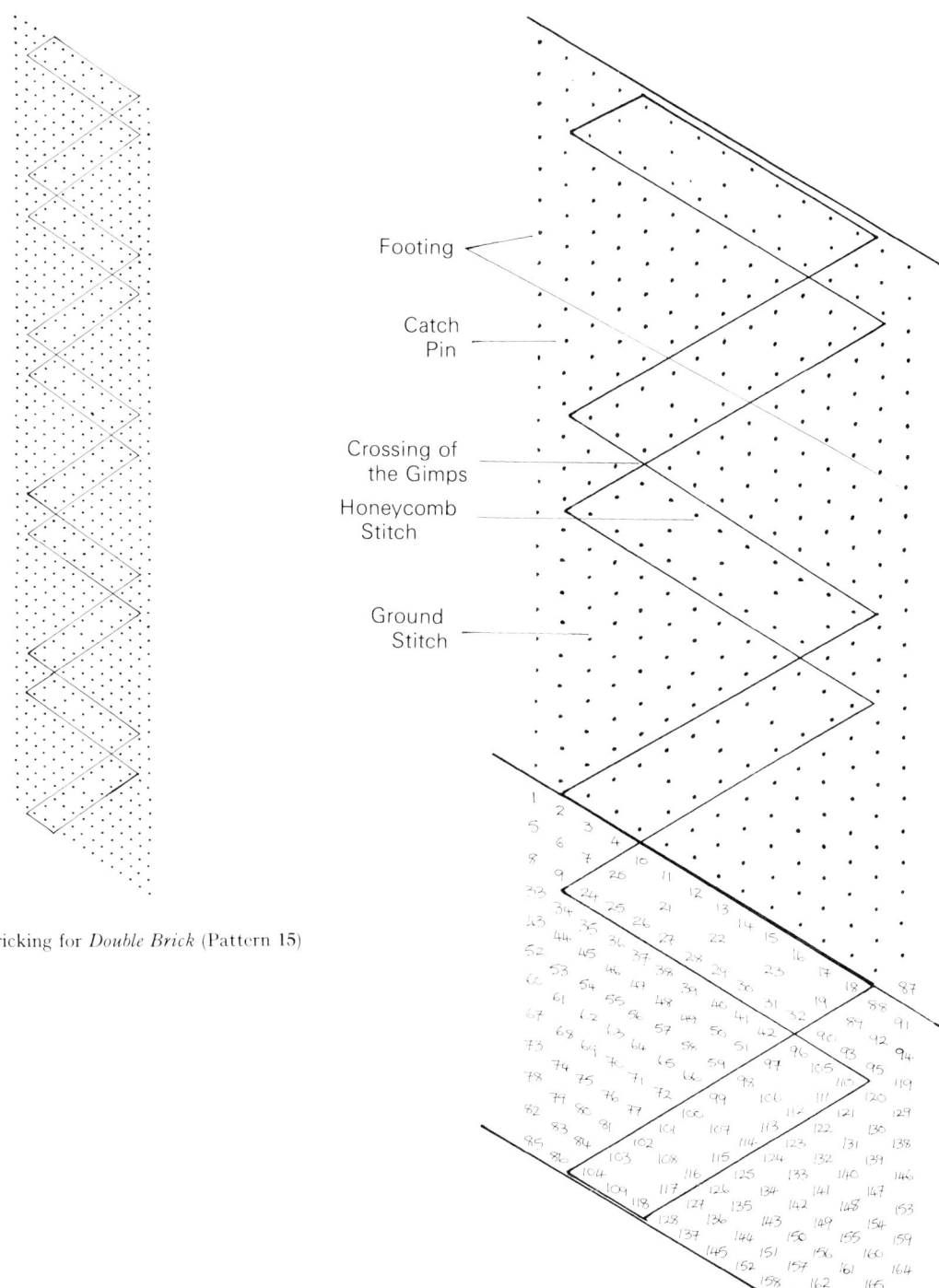

17 Pricking for *Double Brick* (Pattern 15)

Footing

Catch
Pin

Crossing of
the Gimps

Honeycomb
Stitch

Ground
Stitch

18 Technical drawing for *Double Brick* showing the
position of some of the stitches

Church windows

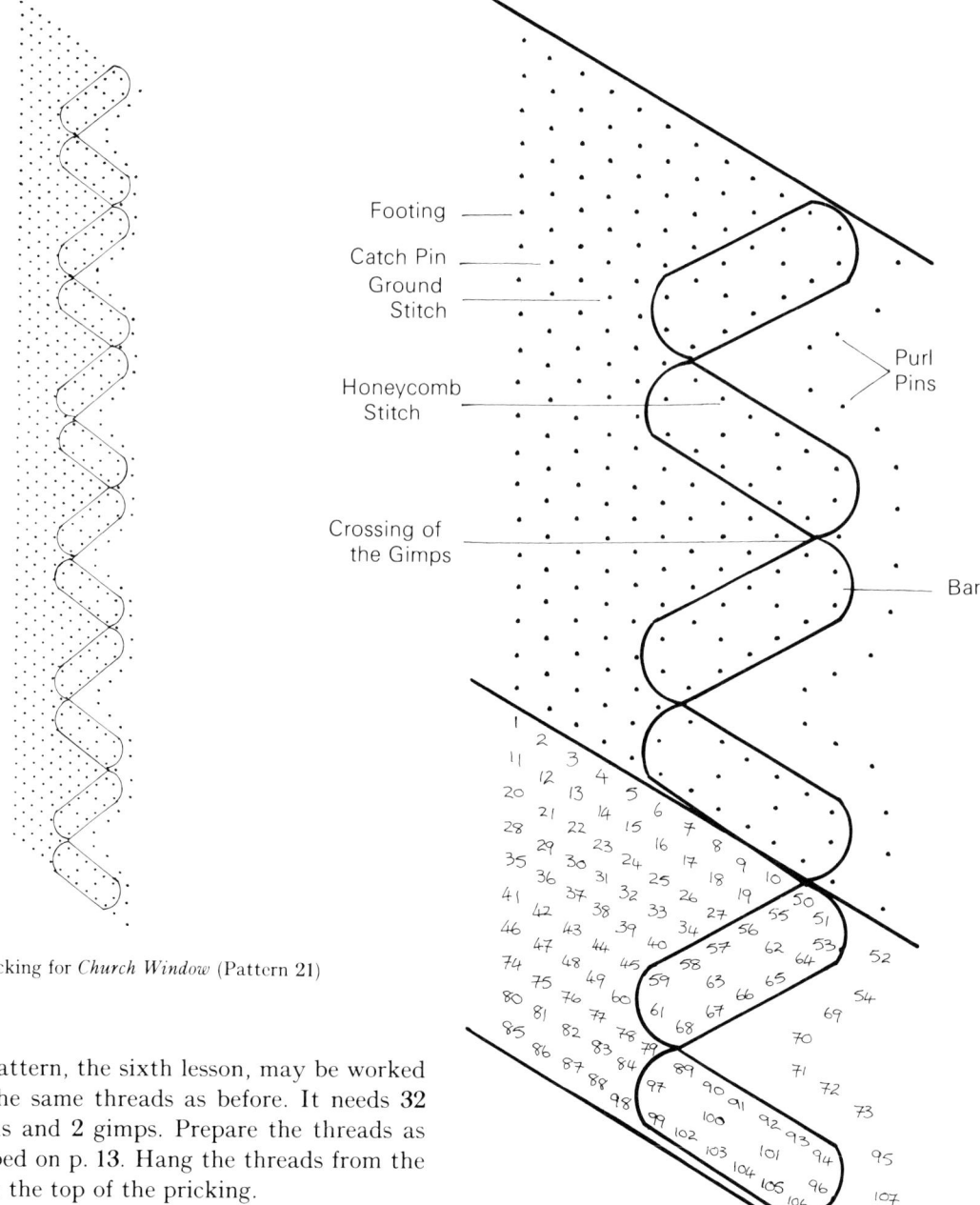

Footing

Catch Pin

Ground Stitch

Honeycomb Stitch

Crossing of the Gimps

Purl Pins

Bar

19 Pricking for *Church Window* (Pattern 21)

This pattern, the sixth lesson, may be worked with the same threads as before. It needs **32** bobbins and **2** gimps. Prepare the threads as described on p. **13**. Hang the threads from the pins at the top of the pricking.

Setting up
a) Start with the foot at pin 1, cp at pin 2, gr st, at pins 3–10. Complete this section until pin 49 is worked.

20 Technical drawing for *Church Window*

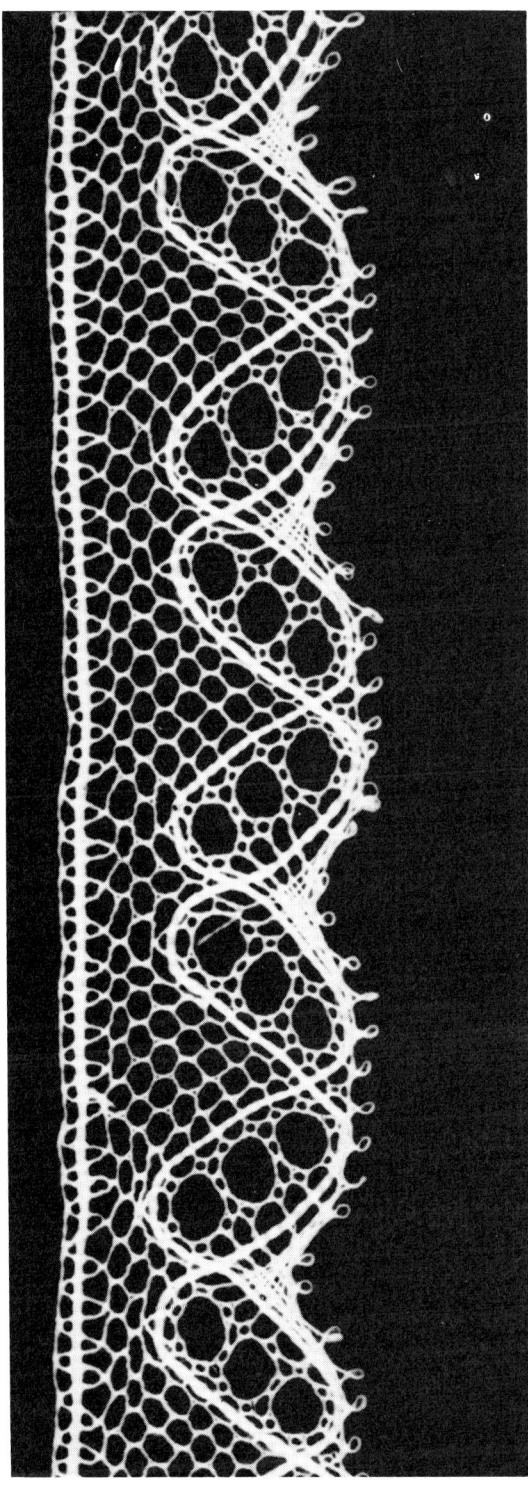

b) Pass the LH gimp through six pairs and the RH gimp through two pairs.

The window

a) With the centre pairs work a hc st, pin and close at pin 50. Pass a pair to the right, hc st, pin and close at 51.

b) Pass the RH gimp to the left through one pair and work PP 52. Pass the RH gimp back to the right through one pair, hc st, pin and close at pin 53.

c) Pass the RH gimp to the left through one pair, work PP 54. Pass the RH gimp back to the right.

d) On the LH side work hc st at pins 55–59. Pass the LH gimp to the right through one pair and work a reverse cp at pin 60.

e) Pass the LH gimp to the left through one pair. Work a hc st, pin and close at pin 61. Work the separates at pins 62 and 63.

f) On the RH side work hc st at pins 64–67. With the centre pairs work pin 68. Pass the LH gimp to the right through two pairs and the RH gimp to the left through five pairs. Cross the gimps.

g) Work PP 69–73.

h) Return to the footing and work pins 74–88. Pass the LH gimp to the left through two pairs and the RH gimp to the right through six pairs. With the two centre pairs start to work the other window.

i) Work pins 89–94. Pass the RH gimp to the left through one pair. Work PP 95. Pass the RH gimp back to the right and work pin 96.

j) On the LH side work pin 97. Pass the LH gimp to the right through one pair and work the reverse cp at pin 98. Work the separates at 100 and 101.

k) Pass the LH gimp to the left through one pair and work pin 99. Work pins 102–105 and using the centre pairs pin 106. Pass the LH gimp to the right through six pairs and the RH gimp to the left through two pairs. Cross the gimps.

l) Work PP 107–109. Pass these pairs through the RH gimp ready to work the next heading.

This completes the instructions for the heading.

Duke's Garter

The seventh lesson is worked in the threads already suggested, requiring 40 bobbins and 2 gimps. You will notice that only two pairs of bobbins are used in most of the heading. As the edge of the pattern is curved, you will see there is a small cl st area in the 'dip'.

Setting up
a) Start with the ft at the LH side, pin 1, the cp, pin 2, and the gr st at pins 3–6. Finish working this area until pin 18 is completed. Pass the RH gimp through four pairs and the LH gimp through four pairs.
b) With the two centre pairs cl st, pin and close at pin 19. Finish working the diamond in numerical order until pin 30 has been worked.

c) Pass the LH gimp to the right through eight pairs. Cross the gimps. Work the gr st at pins 31–34. Return to the footing. Work pins 35 and 36. Work the gr st at 37–41.
d) Pass the LH gimp through five pairs and the RH gimp through five pairs. With the centre pairs work a hc st, pin and close at pin 42. Work pins 43–46 in the same way.
e) Pass the RH gimp to the left through one pair. Work PP 47. Pass the RH gimp back to the right. Work pin 48.
f) Pass the RH gimp to the left through one pair. Work PP 49. With the left centre pair and the pair on the left work a hc st, pin and close at pin 50. Work the separates at pin 51.
g) Work pins 52–56, 57, and the separates at

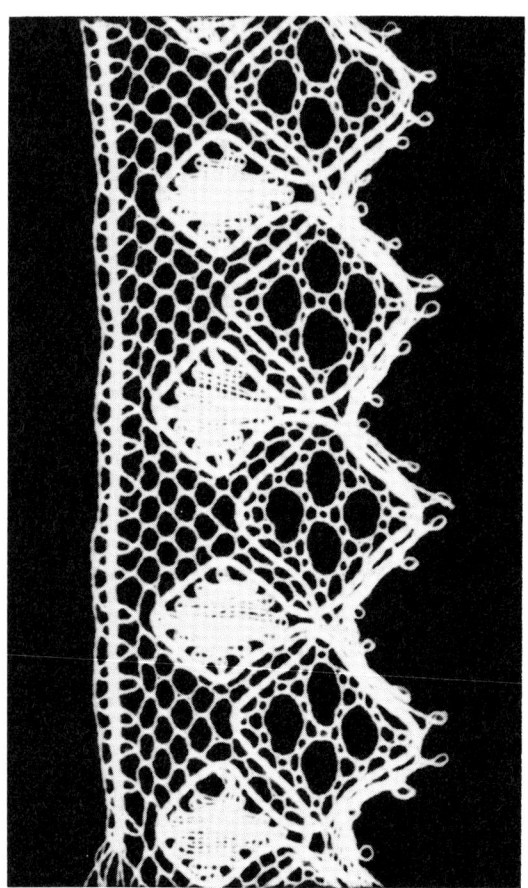

22 *Duke's Garter*

23 *Duke's Garter* (Pattern 108)

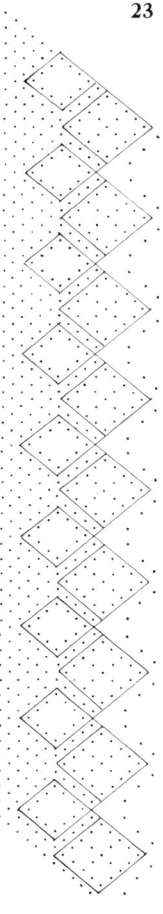

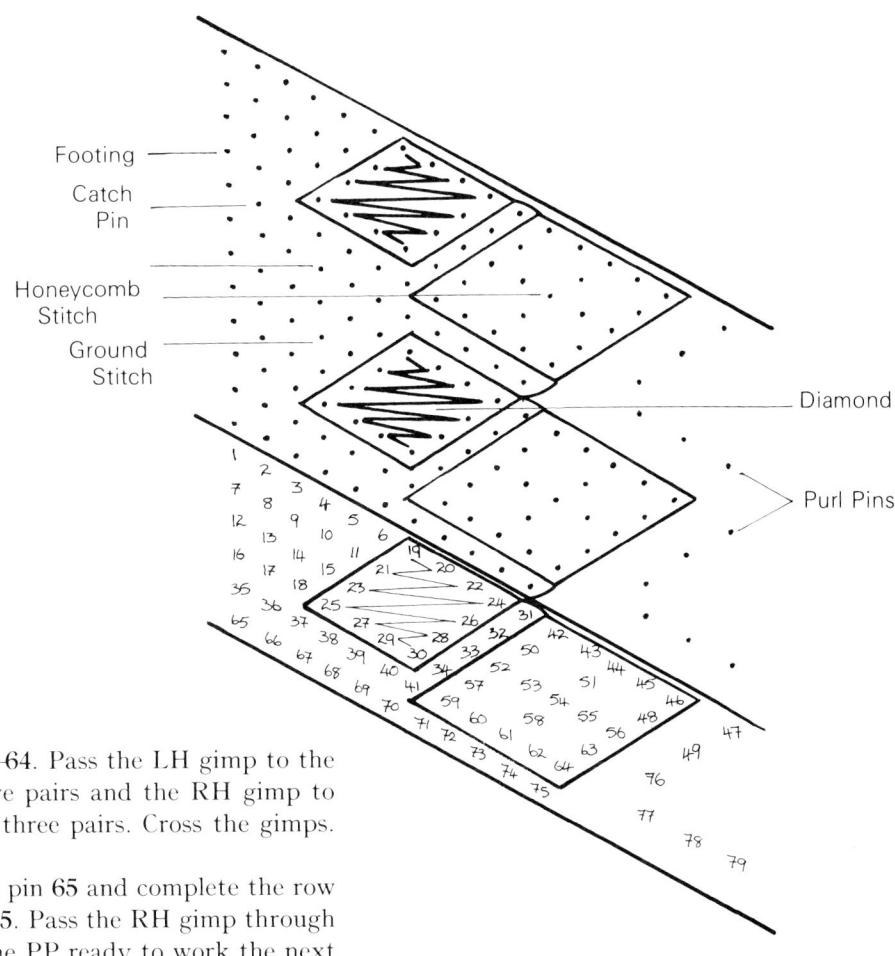

Footing

Catch Pin

Honeycomb Stitch

Ground Stitch

Diamond

Purl Pins

24 Technical drawing for *Duke's Garter*, showing movement of the gimp

pins **58** and **63**.

h) Work pins **59–64**. Pass the LH gimp to the right through five pairs and the RH gimp to the left through three pairs. Cross the gimps. Work PP **76–79**.

i) Work the ft at pin **65** and complete the row finishing at pin **75**. Pass the RH gimp through the pairs from the PP ready to work the next heading.

This completes the instructions for the heading.

The Bean

The eighth pattern introduces another feature – a cloth stitch motif in the form of a bean. The same threads will be used as already suggested, 28 bobbins and 2 gimps. You will notice that a reverse cp is worked at each side of the bean, pins **16** and **49**.

Setting up

a) Start at the LH edge, by starting at pin **1**, cp at pin **2**, and gr st at pins **3–5**. Complete the area, finishing at pin **12**.

b) Pass the LH gimp through two pairs and the RH gimp through four pairs. With the two centre pairs work a cl st, pin and close at pin **13**. Using the same stitch work pins **14** and **15**.

c) Pass the LH gimp to the right, and work the reverse cp at pin **16**. Pass the gimp back to the left, and with the pair from pin **15** cl st to the right and work pin **17**. Work to the left and close at pin **18**.

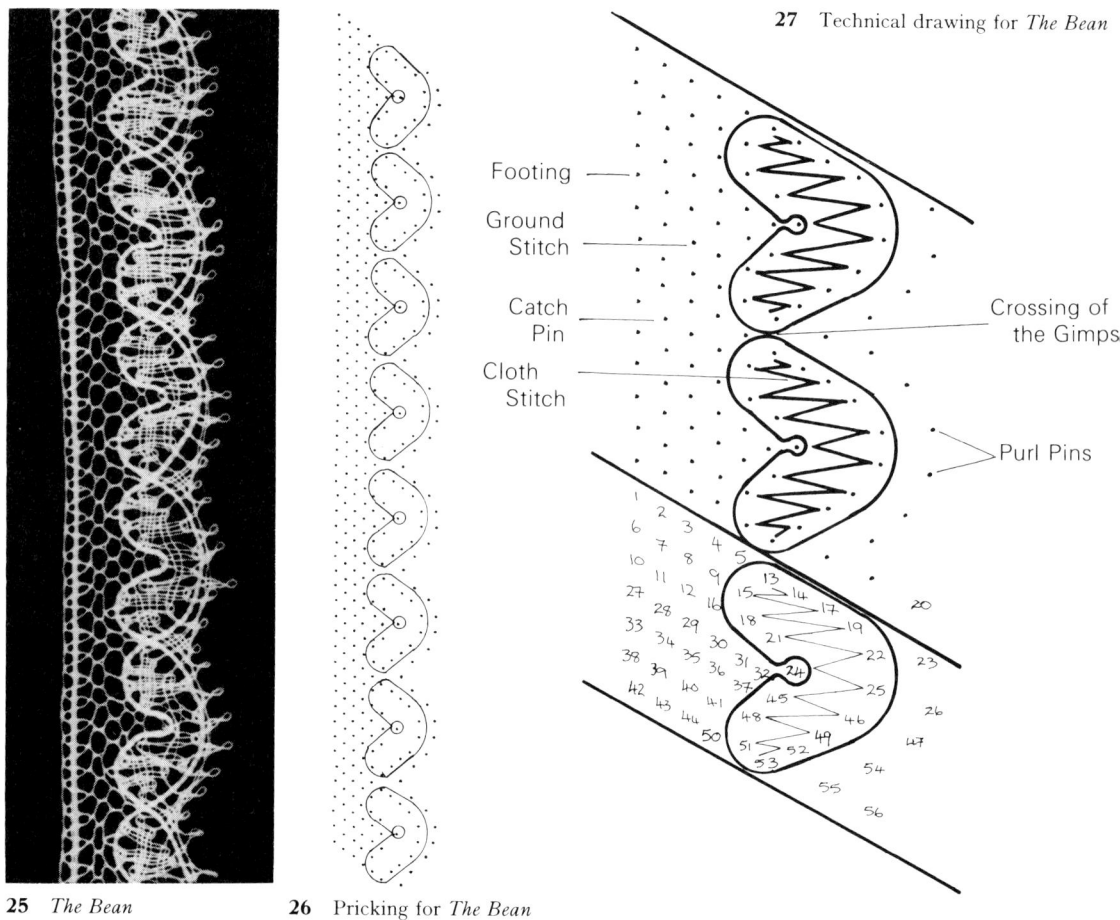

27 Technical drawing for *The Bean*

Footing

Ground Stitch

Catch Pin

Cloth Stitch

Crossing of the Gimps

Purl Pins

25 *The Bean*   **26** Pricking for *The Bean*

d) Pass the LH gimp to the right through one pair. Cl st to the right and close the pin at pin 19. Pass the RH gimp to the left through one pair, work PP 20.

e) Pass the RH gimp to the right through one pair. Using the worker pair from pin 19, cl st to the left. Pin and close at pin 21, cl st to the right and close at pin 22.

f) Pass the gimp through one pair to the left, work PP 23. Pass the RH gimp to the right and cl st to the left. Pass the LH gimp through the worker pair. Two twists, support the pair about the pin at pin 24. Pass the gimp back and cl st to the right. Close at pin 25, work PP 26.

g) Return to the LH edge and work ft pin at pin 27, cp at pin 28 and gr st 29–31. Complete this area, until pin 44 has been worked.

h) Pass the LH gimp through three pairs. Using the worker pair from pin 25, cl st to the left. Pin and close at pin 45. Cl st to the right. Pin and close at pin 46. Pass the RH gimp to the left and work PP 47.

i) Pass the RH gimp back and cl st to the left, closing at pin 48, cl st to the right, closing at pin 49. Cl st to the left and leave. Pass the LH gimp back to the right through one pair.

j) Work a reverse cp at pin 50. Pass the LH gimp back and work pin 51. Cl st to the right and close at pins 52 and 53.

k) Pass the LH gimp through two pairs and the RH gimp through four pairs. Cross the gimps.

l) Work PP 54–56. Pass RH gimp through the pairs from the PP, ready to work the next heading.

This completes the instructions for the heading.

GROUP TWO:

Intermediate

Within this group will be found a variety of Downton features. Amongst the patterns you will find an insertion. On one of the edgings, a different heading has been introduced. A finer thread will also be used in this group of patterns.

Pattern 52

The two threads which have previously been used will be needed for this pattern, 44 bobbins and 2 gimps, to work this insertion.

Setting up
a) Start at the LH edge by working the ft at pin 1, the cp at pin 2, and the gr st at pins 3–5. Complete this area in numerical order, finishing after pin 15 has been worked.

Right-hand side
Repeat as above, working in numerical order.

The centre pattern
a) Work a hc st, pin and close at pin 16. Bring the LH gimp through the pairs from pin 16 and through four more pairs. Work pins 17–20, hc st.
b) Pass the LH gimp to the right through one pair and work the reverse cp at pin 21.
c) Pass the LH gimp to the left through one pair. Work pin 22 and the separates at pins 23–25.
d) Now work the RH side of the diamond. Work a hc st, pin and close at pin 26. Pass the gimp through six pairs and work pins 27–30.
e) Pass the RH gimp to the left through one pair and work the cp at pin 31. Pass the gimp back and work the hc st at pin 32.
f) Work the separates at pins 33–35.

The diamond
a) To work the diamond, work a cl st, pin and close at pin 36. Work to the right and close at pin 37. Finish working the diamond until the two centre pairs have been worked at pin 47.
b) Work the RH side pins at 48–50, and 51–53, Work the LH side pins 54–56. Return to the LH side and complete pins 57–59.
c) Pass the LH gimp through six pairs. Twist each pair three times.
d) Pass the RH gimp through six pairs. Twist each pair three times.
   This complete the instructions for the heading.

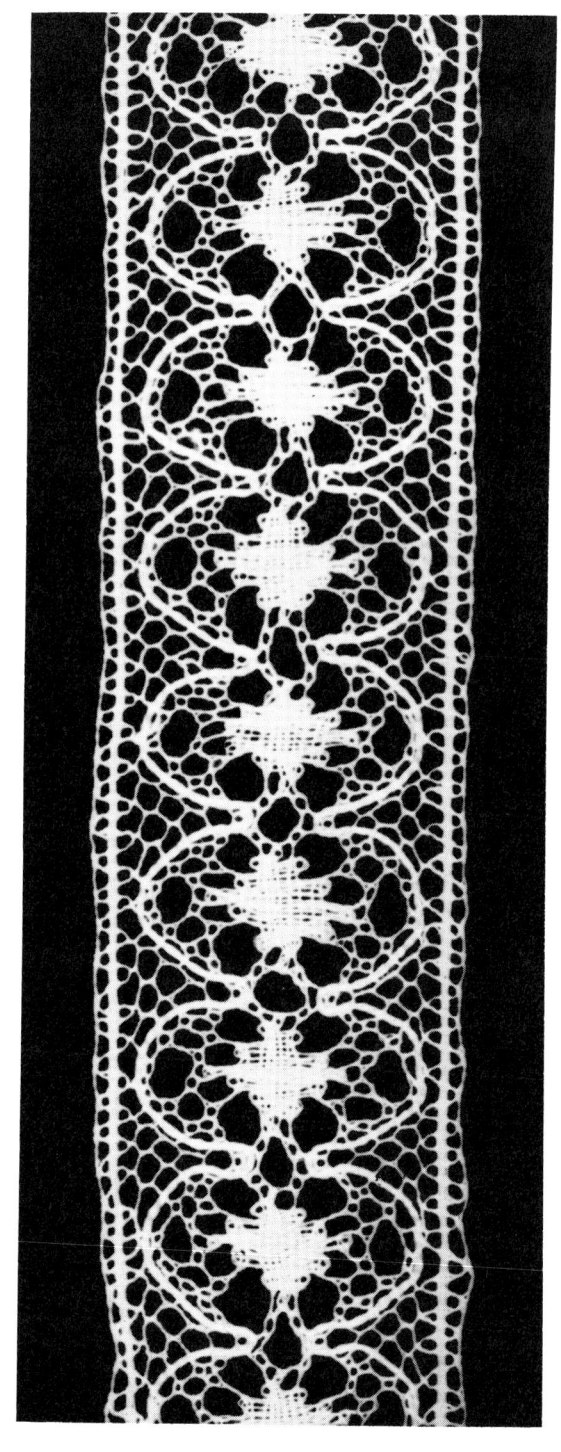

28 Pattern 52, an insertion

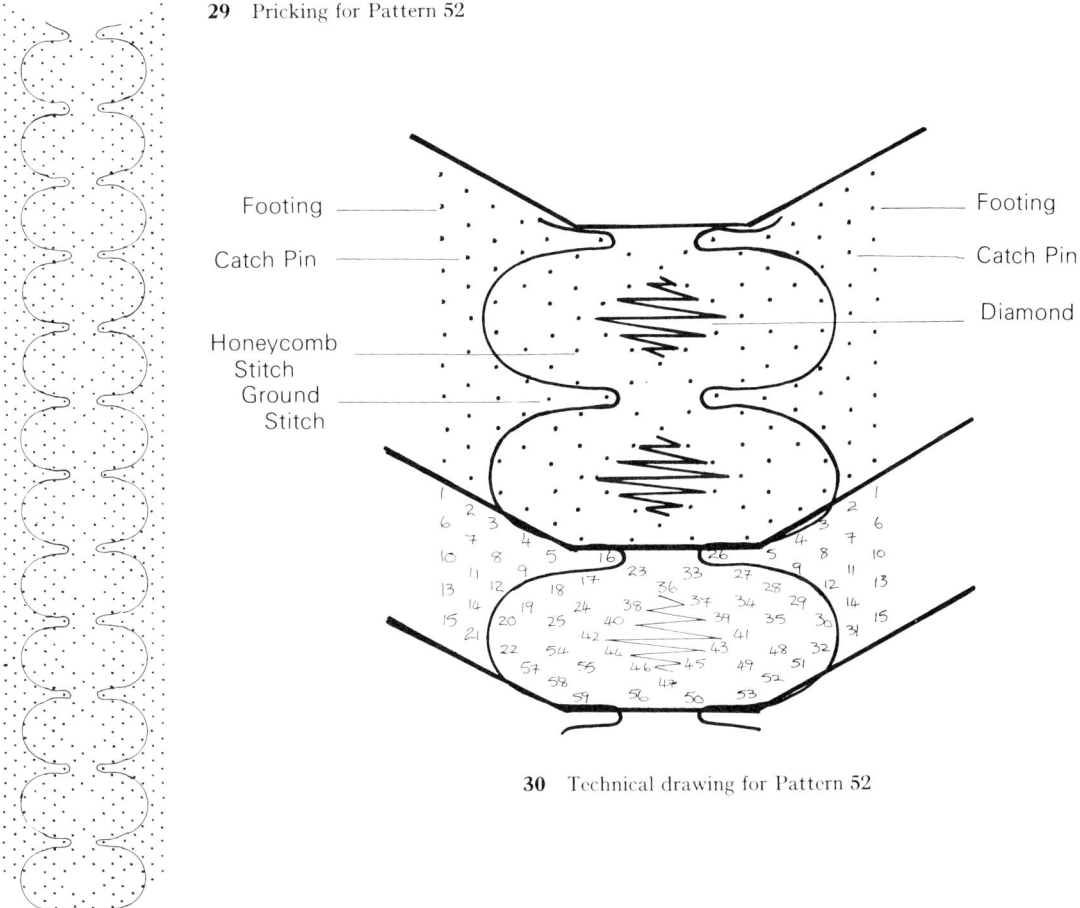

29 Pricking for Pattern 52

Footing

Catch Pin

Diamond

Honeycomb
Stitch
Ground
Stitch

30 Technical drawing for Pattern 52

The Iron (Pattern 50)

This pattern is worked in the usual threads. 32 bobbins and 2 gimps will be needed. Prepare the threads as described on p. 13 and place them at the top of the pricking.

Setting up

a) Start at the foot by working pin 1, the cp at pin 2, and the gr st at pins 3–9. Complete this area, working in numerical order until pin 35 has been worked.

b) Pass the LH gimp through three pairs and the RH gimp through two pairs. Using the two centre pairs work a hc st, pin and close at pins 36–38.

c) At the LH side pass the gimp round and work pin 39 in a hc st. Note that two twists are made on the two RH pairs. Work pin 40.

d) Pass the RH gimp to the right through one pair and work PP 41. Pass the gimp back and work pins 42 and 43.

e) Pass the LH gimp to the left through three pairs. Work pins 44 and 45 in hc st.

f) Pass the LH gimp to the right through three

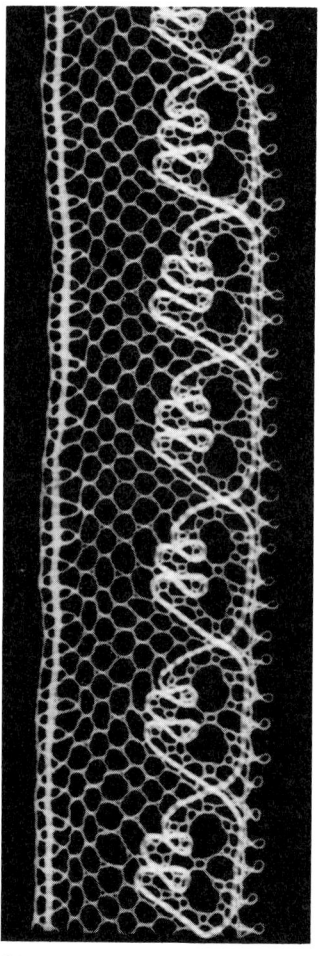

31 *The Iron*

32 Pricking for *The Iron*

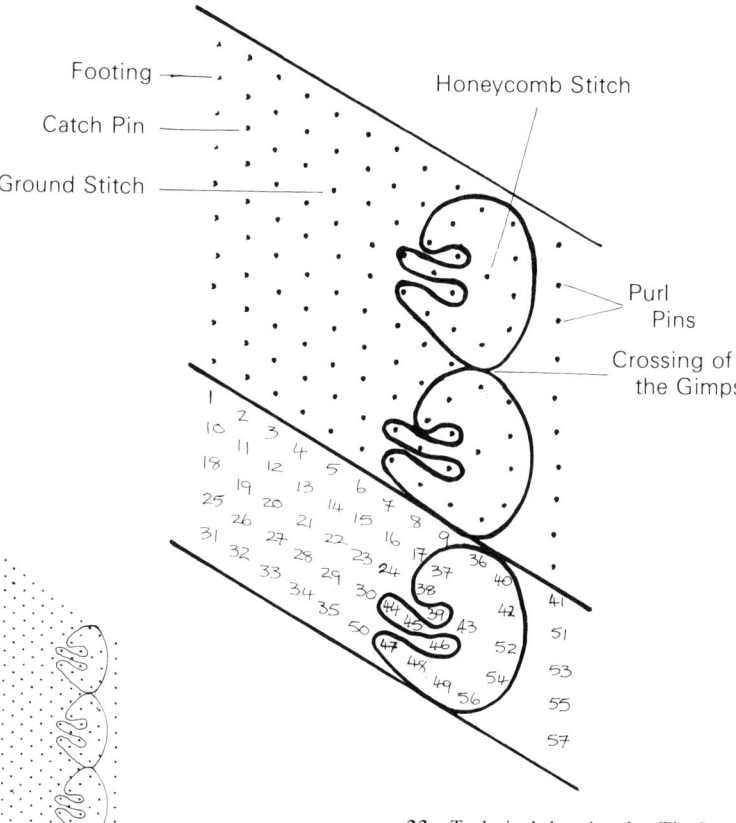

Footing

Catch Pin

Ground Stitch

Honeycomb Stitch

Purl
Pins

Crossing of
the Gimps

33 Technical drawing for *The Iron*

pairs. Work pin 46 in hc st. Work pin 50 in gr st.

g) Pass the LH gimp to the left through four pairs and work pins 47–49 in hc st. When two gimps pass together there are no twists between the gimps.

h) Pass the RH gimp to the left through one pair. Work PP 51. Pass the gimp back, remembering to make the appropriate twists ready for the next stitch.

i) Work pin 52, PP 53, pin 54, PP 55.

Using the centre pairs work pin 56. Work PP 57 with the RH pair from the centre pin. Pass the LH gimp through four pairs. Cross the gimps.

This completes the instructions for the heading.

The Ace of Diamonds

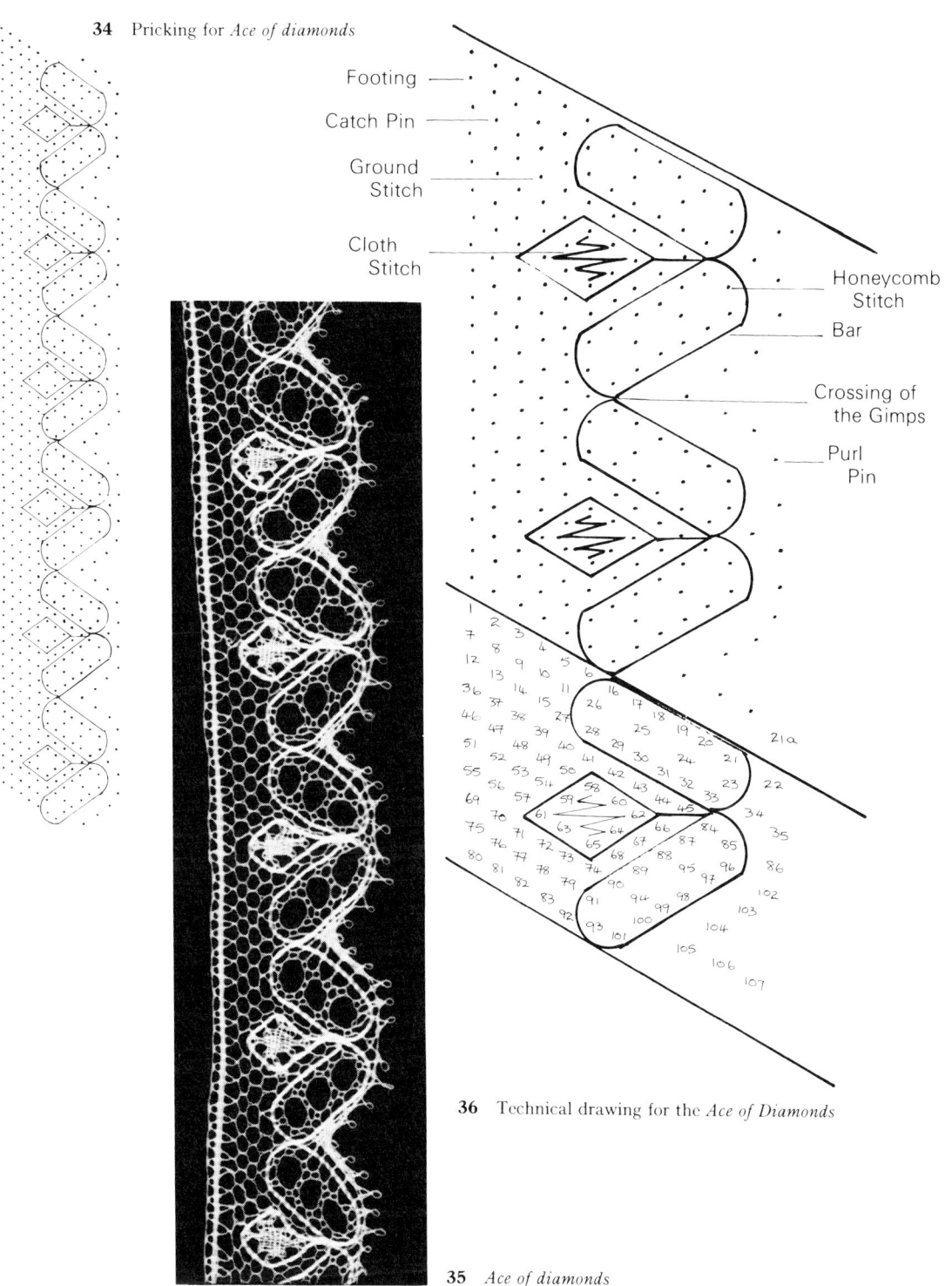

34 Pricking for *Ace of diamonds*

Footing

Catch Pin

Ground Stitch

Cloth Stitch

Honeycomb Stitch

Bar

Crossing of the Gimps

Purl Pin

36 Technical drawing for the *Ace of Diamonds*

35 *Ace of diamonds*

This pattern is built up of bars, diamonds, and a curved edge. In the 'dip' you will find a small area of cl st. Between the two bars at the outer edge note the pin. This is a hc st. Two reverse cp are worked at the tips of the bars. The same threads as before, are needed for this pattern, 32 bobbins and 2 gimps.

Setting up
Prepare the threads as described on p. 13.

The bar
a) Start at the ft working pin 1, the cp at pin 2, and the gr st pins 3–6. Complete this area working in numerical order until pin 15 has been worked.
b) Pass the LH gimp to the left through two pairs and the RH gimp to the right through five pairs. Make two twists on each pair. Work hc st at pins 16–20. Pass the RH gimp to the left and work PP 21a. Pass the gimp back and work pin 21.
c) Pass the RH gimp through one pair to the left and work PP 22. Pass the RH gimp back to the right and work pin 23.
d) Work the separates at pins 24 and 25. Work pin 26. Pass the LH gimp to the right through one pair. Three twists should be applied to this pair.
e) Work the reverse cp at pin 27. Pass the LH gimp to the left through one pair and work pins 28–33. Pass the LH gimp to the right.
f) Pass the RH gimp to the left and work the hc st at pin 34. Work PP 35. Cross the gimps.
g) Return to the footing and working in numerical order complete pins 36–57.

Pass the LH gimp to the left through eight pairs.

The diamond
a) Using the two centre pairs cl st pin and close at pin 58. Working in numerical order complete the diamond finishing at pin 65. Pass the LH gimp to the right through eight pairs. Work pins 66–68 in gr st.
b) Return to the footside and working in numerical order complete pins 69–83. Cross the gimps.
c) Pass the LH gimp to the left through six pairs and the RH gimp to the right through two pairs.

The bar
a) Using the two centre pairs work the hc st at pins 84 and 85. Pass the RH gimp to the left through one pair. Work PP 86 (see Fig. 36).
b) On the LH side of this bar work pins 87–91.
c) Pass the LH gimp to the right through one pair. Work the reverse cp at pin 92.
d) Pass the LH gimp to the left through one pair and work the hc st at pin 93.
e) Work the separates at pins 94 and 95.
f) On the RH side of the bar work pins 96–100 (hc st). Complete the bar by working pin 101 with the two centre pairs.
g) Pass the LH gimp through two pairs and the RH gimp through five pairs. Cross the gimps.
h) Work PP 102–107. Pass the RH gimp through the pairs used to work the PP, ready to work the next heading.
  These instructions complete the heading.

Pattern 186

This pattern brings together a variety of features used in Downton Lace. You will see that this edging has a straight heading, decorated with purl pins. In the centre, you will find 'fingers', a diamond, and the hc st filling. The gimp threads are used to produce an elaborate design. Care should be taken to cross the gimps in the places indicated.

Prepare the threads as described on p. 13 and place them at the top of the pricking. The same threads are used to work this pattern, 34 bobbins and 2 gimps.

Setting up
a) Start at the footing by working pin 1, the cp at pin 2, and gr st and pins 3–8.

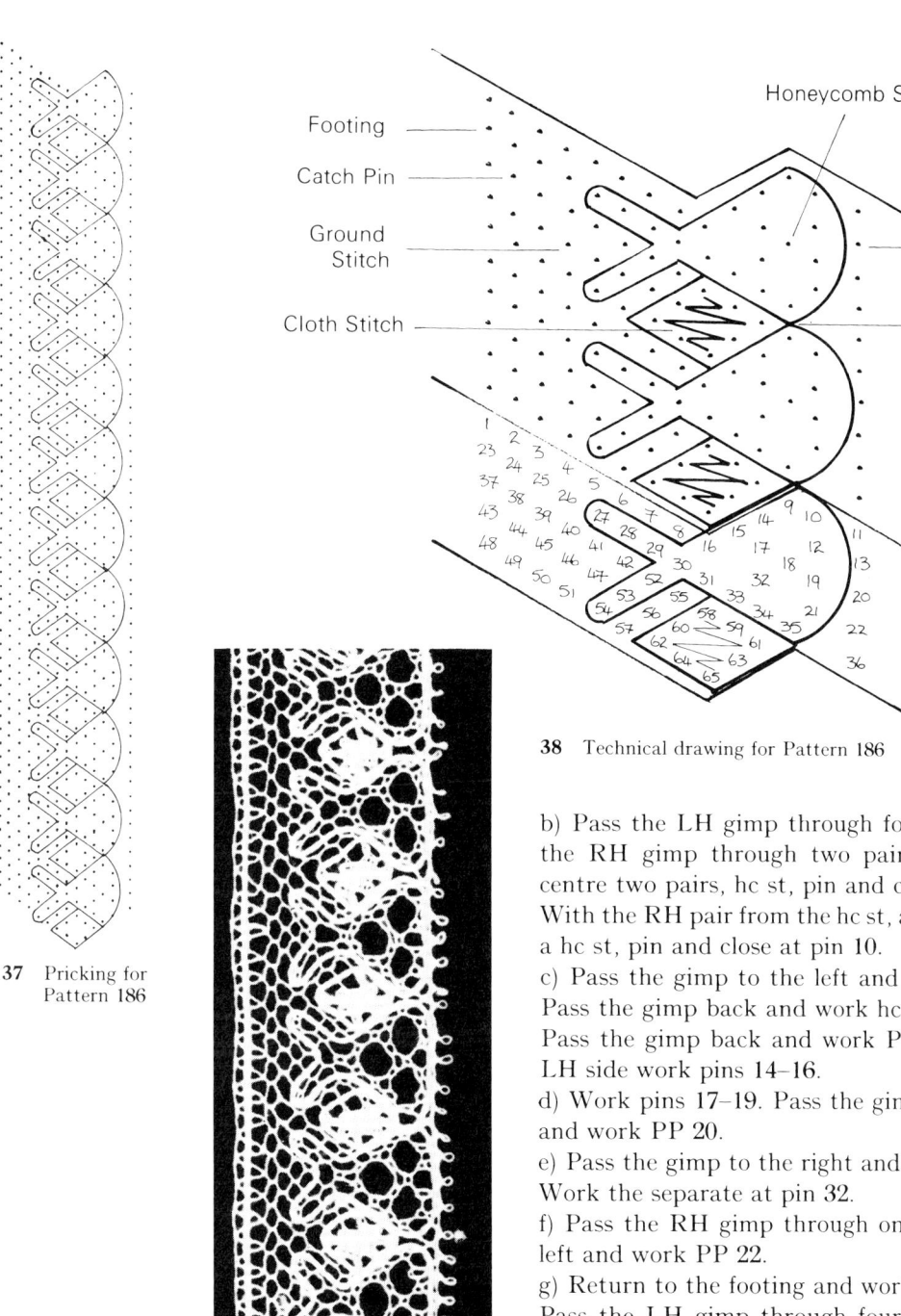

37 Pricking for Pattern 186

38 Technical drawing for Pattern 186

39 Pattern 186

b) Pass the LH gimp through four pairs, and the RH gimp through two pairs. Using the centre two pairs, hc st, pin and close at pin 9. With the RH pair from the hc st, at pin 9, work a hc st, pin and close at pin 10.

c) Pass the gimp to the left and work PP 11. Pass the gimp back and work hc st at Pin 12. Pass the gimp back and work PP 13. On the LH side work pins 14–16.

d) Work pins 17–19. Pass the gimp to the left and work PP 20.

e) Pass the gimp to the right and work pin 21. Work the separate at pin 32.

f) Pass the RH gimp through one pair to the left and work PP 22.

g) Return to the footing and work pins 23–26. Pass the LH gimp through four pairs to the left, and work gr st at pins 27–29. Work hc st at pins 30–34, closing with the two centre pairs at pin 35.

h) Pass the RH gimp to the left and work PP 36. Pass the LH gimp to the right through three pairs.

34

i) Return to the footing and work pins 37–51. Pass the LH gimp to the left through three pairs. Work gr st at pins 52–54.

j) Pass the LH gimp to the right through eight pairs. Cross the gimps. Work gr st at pins 55–57. Pass the LH gimp to the left through six pairs. Work the diamond starting at pin 58. Work in numerical order finishing with the two centre pairs at pin 65. Make one twist on each pair as it is thrown out.

k) Pass the LH gimp to the right through six pairs.

l) Cross the gimps.

This completes the instructions for the heading.

Pattern 67

A tally is used in this pattern. When working a tally, take care to support the twisted pairs on pins. This will help to improve its appearance. The edge is slightly curved, and so there will be a small area of cl st in the 'dip'. A reverse cp is worked at the inner edge of the motif. For this design a 160 cotton and No. 12 DMC Coton Perle was used, 30 bobbins and 2 gimps.

Setting up

a) Start at the ft and work pins 1–18. Pass the LH gimp to the left through two pairs, and the RH gimp to the right through four pairs.

b) With the two centre pairs work a hc st, pin and close at pin 19. With the RH centre pair and the pair on the right work a hc st, pin and close at pin 20. Complete pins 21 and 22 in the same way.

c) Pass the RH gimp to the left and work PP 23. Put the RH gimp to the right through one pair and work pin 24. Work the separates at pin 25. Work pin 26.

d) Pass the LH gimp to the right through one pair, and work the reverse cp at pin 27.

e) Pass the gimp back to the left through one pair and work pin 28. Pass the LH gimp to the right through two pairs and work a hc st at pin 29. Before closing the pin, pass the gimp to the left through one pair.

f) With the pair on the right, work a hc st, pin and close at pins 30–31. Return to the LH edge and work pins 32–40.

g) Work the tally, and support the threads on pins. The pins can be removed as the pairs are required for working.

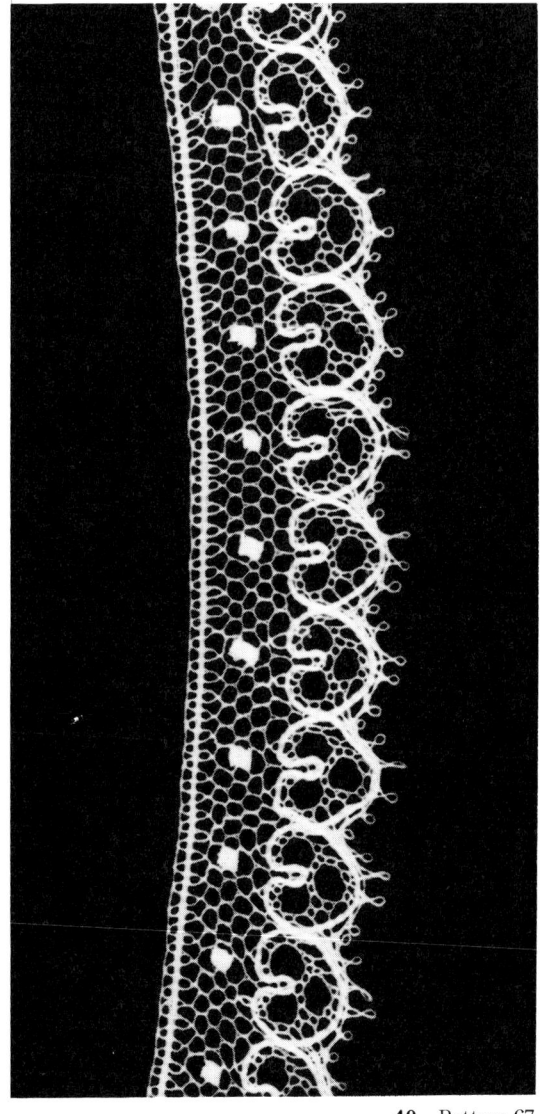

Work the gr st at pin 41.

h) Pass the LH gimp to the left through one pair. Hc st, pin and close at pin 42. Pass the LH gimp to the right through one pair and work the reverse cp at pin 43.

i) Pass the LH gimp back to the left and work pins 44–46. Pass the LH gimp through two pairs and the RH gimp through four pairs.

j) Cross the gimps. Work PP 47–50. Pass the RH gimp through these pairs ready to work the next heading.

These instructions complete the heading.

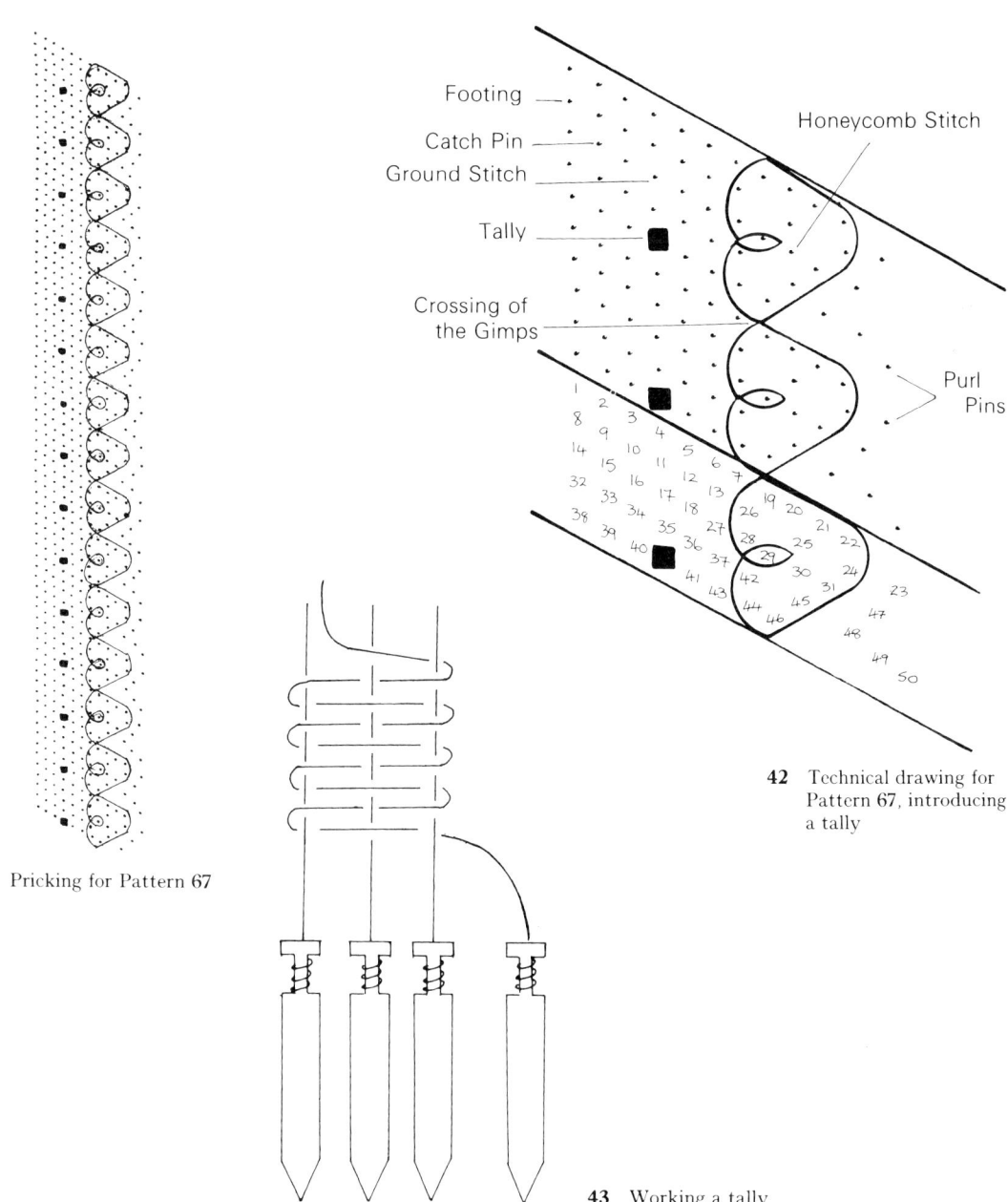

Footing

Catch Pin

Ground Stitch

Tally

Crossing of the Gimps

Honeycomb Stitch

Purl Pins

42 Technical drawing for Pattern **67**, introducing a tally

41 Pricking for Pattern 67

43 Working a tally

Pattern 53

This pattern introduces another edge at the heading. False purl pins are made by putting twists on the worker pair as the threads are passed about the pin. 160 Cotton thread, 32 bobbins, No. 12 DMC Coton Perle, and 1 gimp are required. The 'Downton whole stitch' features in the cloth stitch heading of this pattern.

Setting up
a) Start at the footside by working pin 1, cp at pin 2, and gr st at pins 3–10.
b) Working in numerical order complete the area until pin 24 has been worked. Work the tally and the gr st at pins 25 and 26.
c) Work the ft at pin 27 and complete the area until pin 39 is worked. Pass the gimp through five pairs to the left. Twist each pair once. Find the worker pair at the RH edge. Cl st to the left. Put up the pin at pin 40.
d) Cl st to the right through two pairs, twist the workers once. Cl st, twist the workers once and the passives once. Close the pin at pin 41. Twist each pair.
e) Work in cl st to the left through three pairs. Pin and close at pin 42.
f) Cl st to the right through three pairs and work pin 43 as for pin 41. Twist each pair once.
g) Cl st to the left through four pairs. Pin and close at pin 44. Cl st to the right through four pairs and work pin 45 as for pin 41.
h) Cl st to the left through five pairs and close the pin at pin 46. Cl st to the right through five pairs and work pin 47 as for pin 41.
i) Cl st to the left through five pairs and close the pin at pin 48. Cl st to the right through four pairs and close the pin at pin 49 as for pin 41.
j) Cl st to the left through five pairs and close the pin at pin 50. Cl st to the right through four pairs and work pin 51 as before.
k) Cl st to the left through four pairs. Pin and close at pin 52. Cl st to the right through three pairs and work pin 53 as before.
l) Cl st to the left through three pairs. Pin and close at pin 54. Cl st to the right through three pairs and work pin 55 as before.

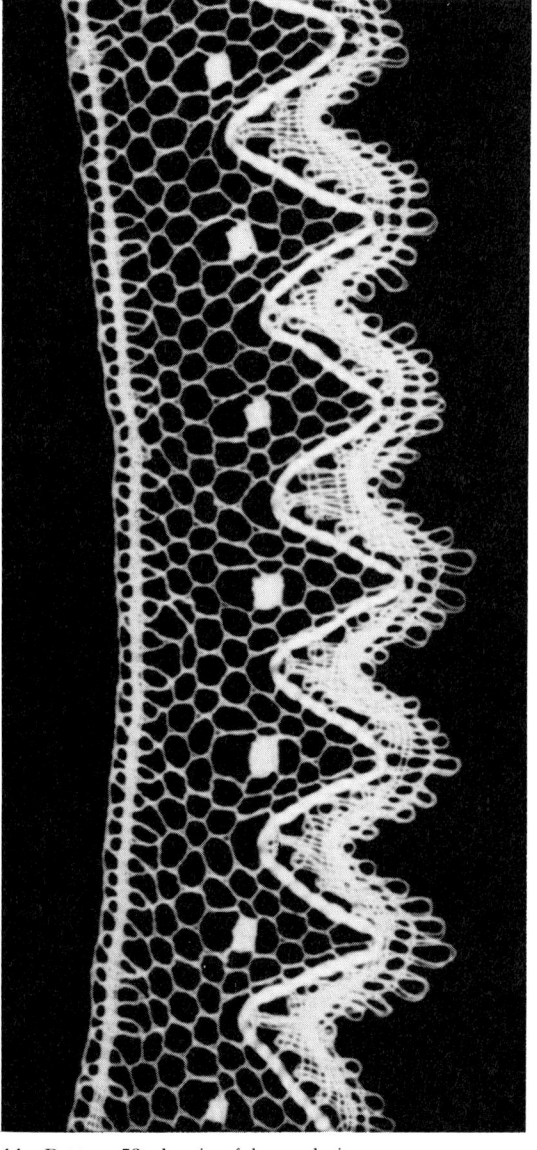

44   Pattern 53, showing false purl pins

m) Cl st to the left through two pairs. Pin and close at pin 56. Cl st to the right through two pairs and work pin 57 as before. Twist the thrown-out pairs once. Pass the gimp to the right through five pairs and twist each pair three times.

This completes the instructions for the heading.

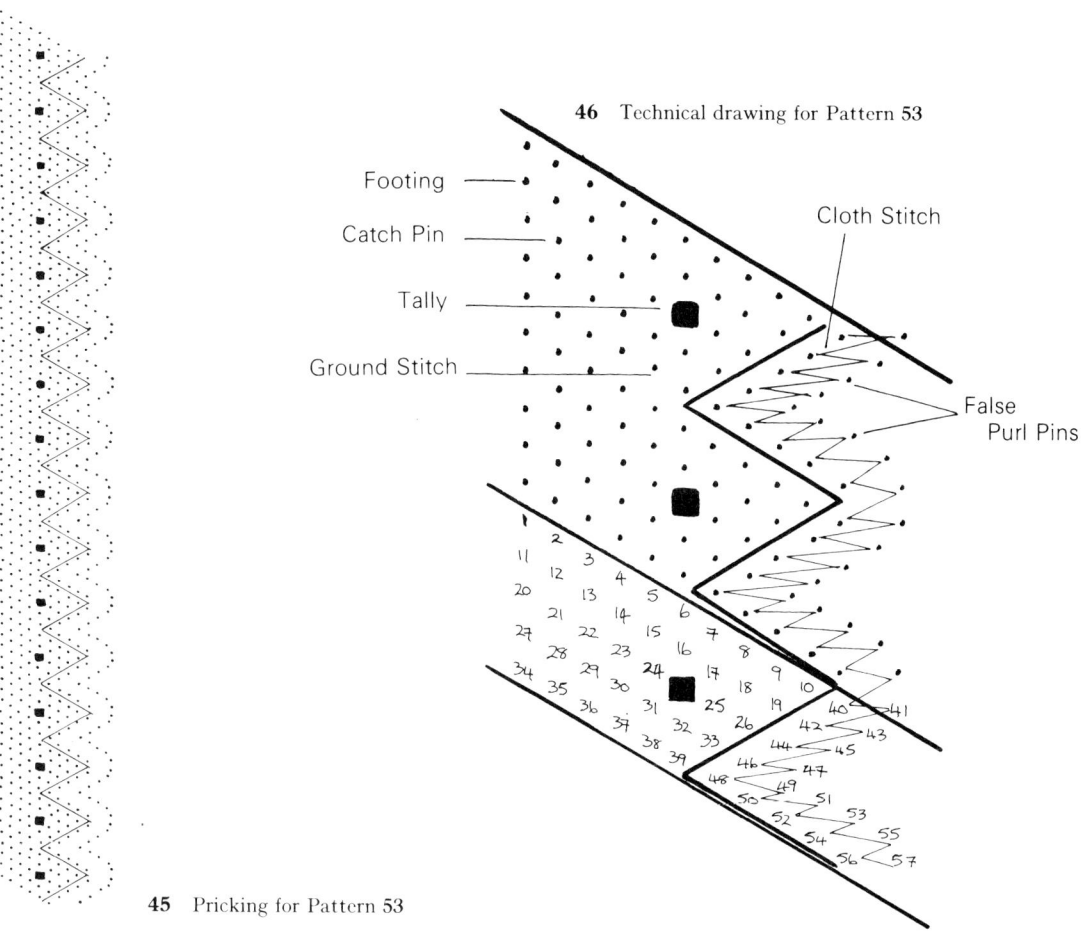

46 Technical drawing for Pattern 53

Footing

Catch Pin

Tally

Ground Stitch

Cloth Stitch

False
Purl Pins

45   Pricking for Pattern 53

The Cheese Cutter

In this section several gimp threads are used in one pricking. Care must be taken, by constant observation of the technical drawings, to ensure that they cross and move in the correct direction. It is most important not to overlook the position, if any, of the reverse catchpin stitches, as they are easily forgotten. 120 Cotton thread, 48 bobbins, No. 12 DMC Coton Perle, 4 gimps.

Setting up
a) Start at the foot, pin 1, and work the area pins 2–33.

The trail
a) Using the lower pair of gimps, pass the LH gimp to the left through six pairs. Twist each pair twice. Start to work the narrow cl st trail at pin 34.
b) Bring in pairs from the LH side. Throw out one pair at each pin on the RH side. It will be necessary to move the RH gimp to the left to work pin 43. Two twists about the pin are worked at this pin. Finish when pin 44 has been worked (see Fig. 49).
c) Work the separates at pins 45 and 46.
d) Pass the RH gimp (outside gimp), through

six pairs. Pass the LH gimp to the left through three pairs.

e) Using the two centre pairs, work a hc st, pin and close at pin 47. On the LH side work pins 48 and 49, and on the RH side work pins 50–54.

f) Work the separates at pins 55 and 56. Work the LH side of the bar and complete pins 57–60.

g) Pass the LH gimp (outside gimp), to the right through four pairs. Work the separates, pins 61 and 62.

h) Pass the LH gimp (outside gimp), to the left through eight pairs around the diamond.

i) Work the diamond in numerical order. Pass the LH gimp around the lower edge of the diamond. Make the necessary twists before and after passing the gimp.

j) Work the separates, pins 75–78. Pass the RH gimp (outside gimp), through one pair to the left. Work PP 79. Pass the gimp back. Work pin 80.

k) On the LH side (outside gimp), pass the gimp through four pairs. Work pins 81–84, hc st. Work the separates, pins 85–87.

l) On the RH side of the bar work pins 88–91, and close with the centre pairs at pin 92. Work PP 93–98 (see Fig. 49).

m) Pass the RH gimp (inside gimp), through six pairs. Finish working the cl st trail, pins 99–111. Pass the LH gimp (inside gimp), to the right through six pairs.

These instructions complete the heading.

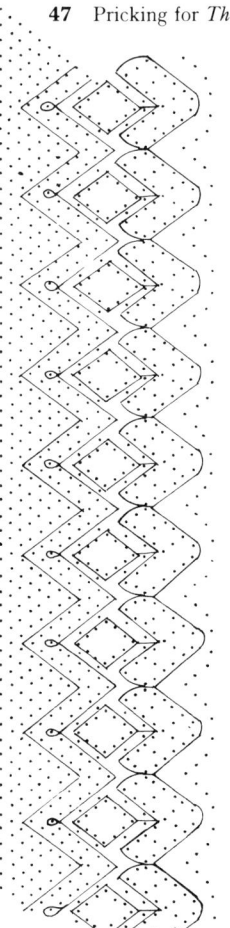

47 Pricking for *The Cheese Cutter*

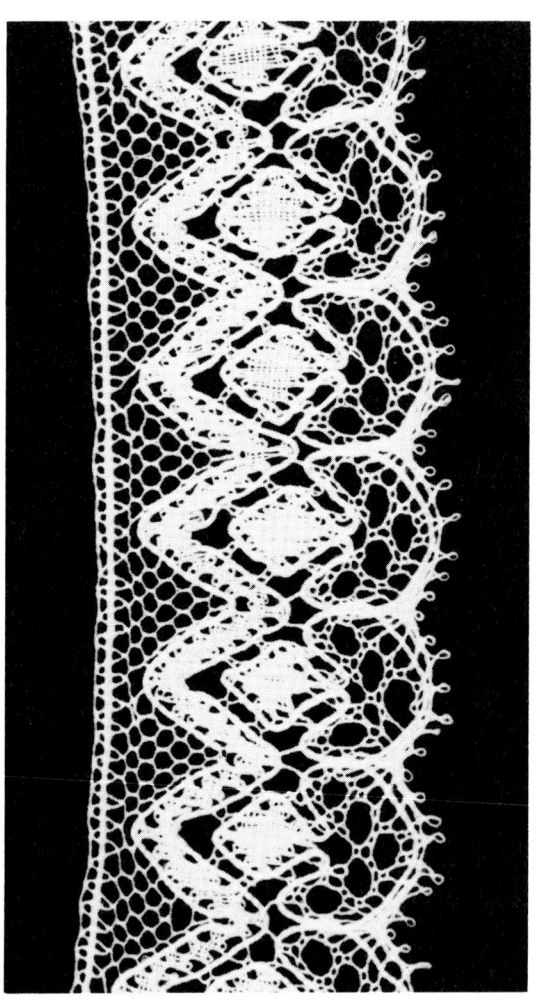

48 *The Cheese Cutter*

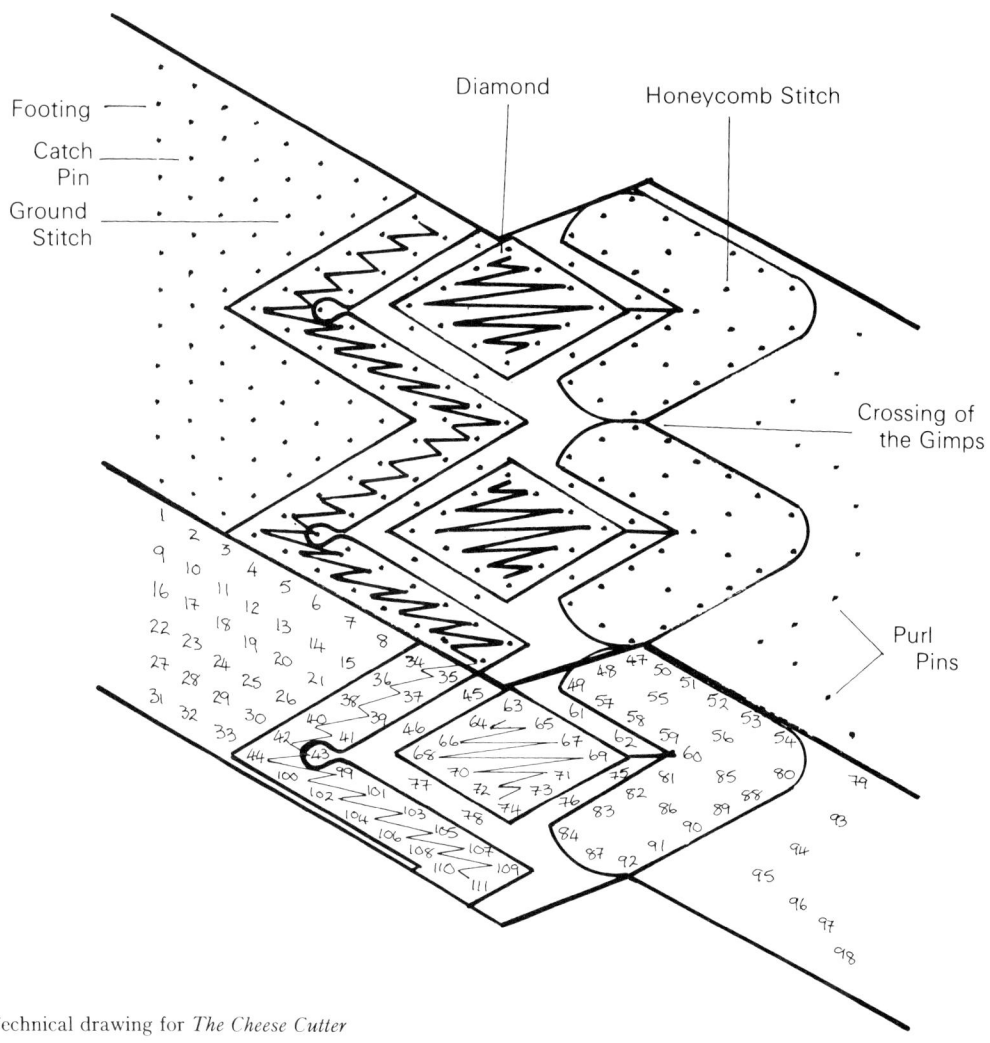

Footing

Catch
Pin

Ground
Stitch

Diamond

Honeycomb Stitch

Crossing of
the Gimps

Purl
Pins

49 Technical drawing for *The Cheese Cutter*

Ace of Clubs

By the time you attempt this pattern you should be familiar with the features of Downton Lace. Close consultation of the technical drawing will show the crossing and movement of the gimps. Do not forget to make the correct number of twists when passing the gimp as the individual stitches are worked. Note that there are two reverse catchpins at pins 42 and 176.

The usual threads are needed to work this pattern, **52** bobbins and **2** gimps.

Setting up
a) Work in numerical order pins 1–29 (the first bar).
Working from the RH side, pass the LH gimp to the left through two pairs and the RH gimp

to the right through six pairs. Using hc st work pins 30–35.

b) Pass the RH gimp to the left through one pair and work PP 36. Pass the gimp back. Work pin 37. Pass the gimp back to the left and work PP 38.

c) Work pins 39–41. Pass the LH gimp to the right and work the reverse catchpin at pin 42.

d) Pass the gimp back to the left and work pins 43–48. Pass the RH gimp through two pairs to the left and work the hc st at pin 49, and PP 50. Pass the LH gimp through six pairs to the right. Cross the gimps. Return to the footside and work pins 51–111 (see Fig. 52).

The club

a) Pass the LH gimp to the left through eleven pairs. Start to work the 'club' at pin 112, finishing at pin 118. Pass the LH gimp to the right through three pairs. With the worker-pair from pin 118, make two twists about the pin. Pass the LH gimp to the left, and work across to pins 120, 121, and 122. Leave.

b) Work the gr st at pins 123–142. Pass the LH gimp to the left around the diamond.

The diamond

a) Work the diamond in numerical order. Pass the LH gimp around the lower edge of the diamond through nine pairs.

b) Work the gr st at pins 151–155, noting that pin 151 is worked with the worker-pair from pin 122.

c) Pass the LH gimp to the left through three pairs. With the worker-pair from pin 151, finish working the 'club'.

d) Pass the LH gimp to the right through ten pairs. Work gr st at pins 164–169. Cross the gimps.

e) Pass the LH gimp through six pairs and the RH gimp to the right through two pairs.

The second bar

a) Work the bar in numerical order. Do not forget to work the PP.

b) Work pins 193–199 in gr st.

These instructions complete the heading.

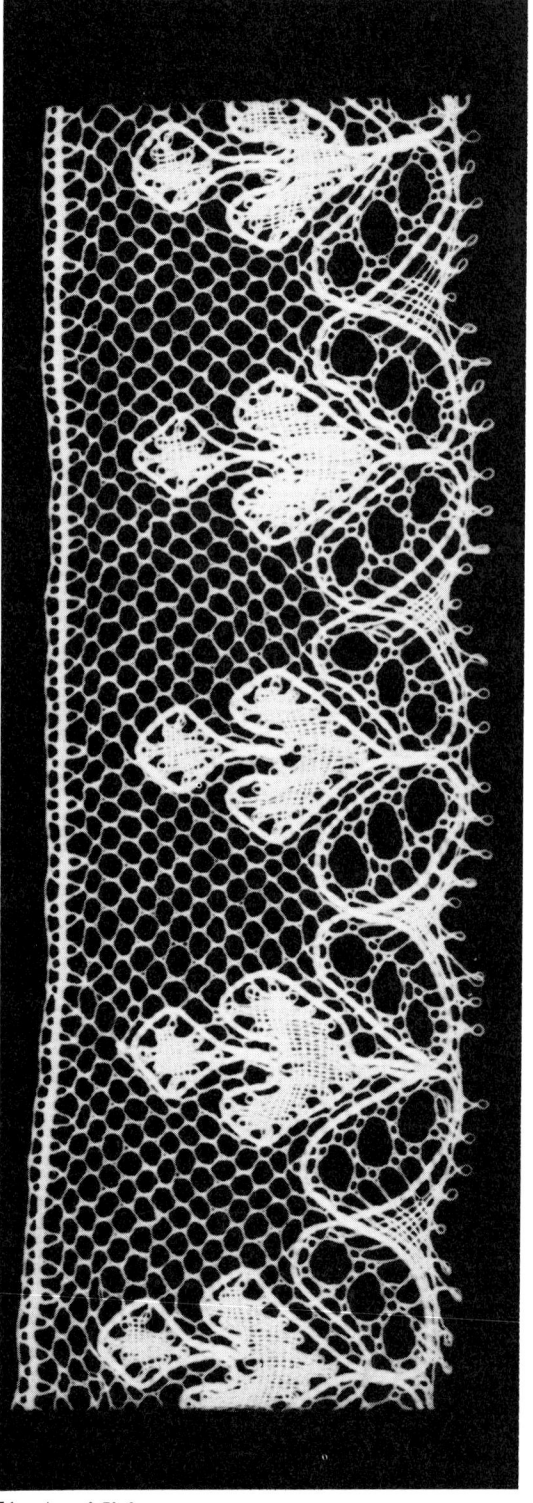

51 *Ace of Clubs*

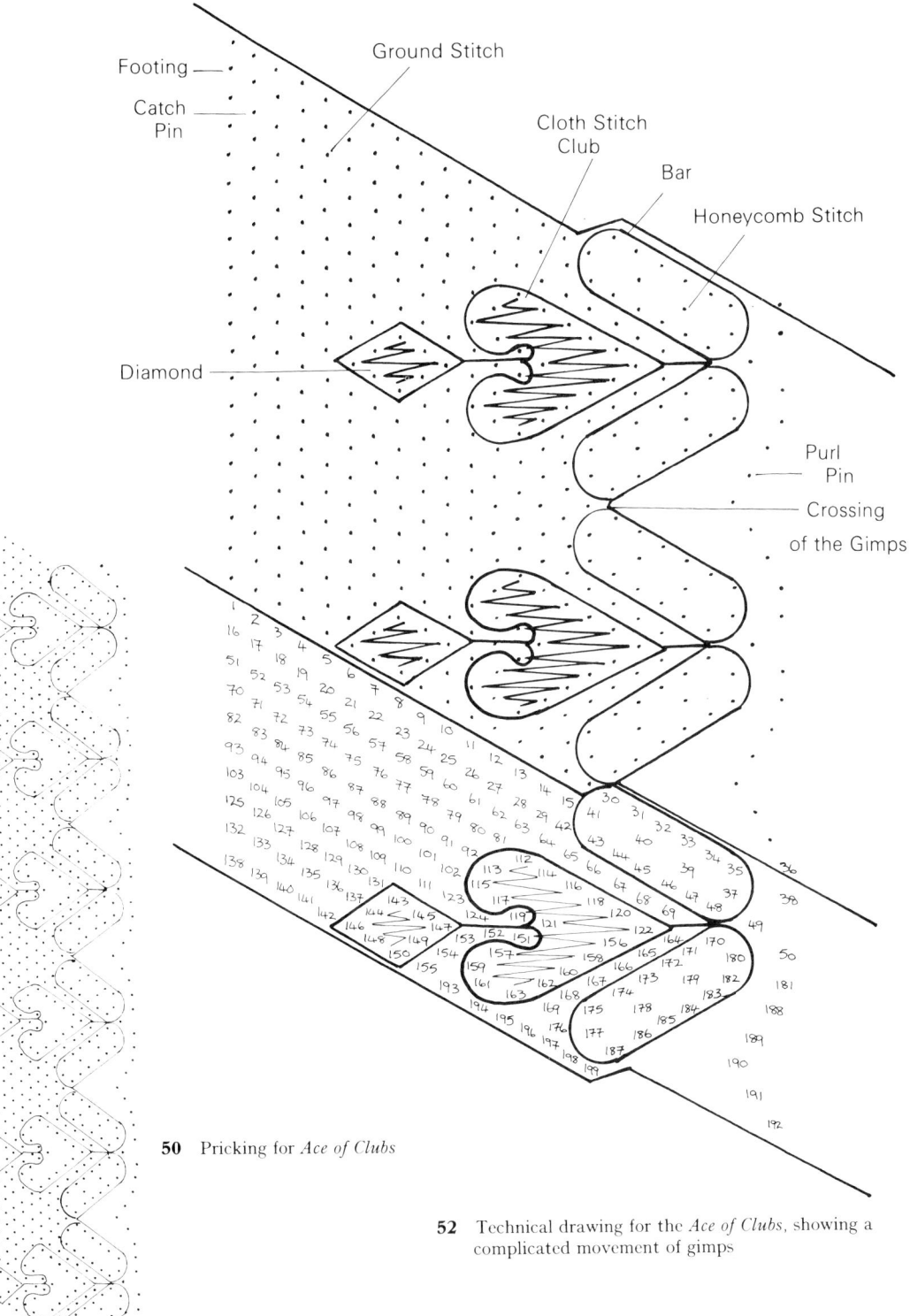

Footing

Ground Stitch

Catch Pin

Cloth Stitch Club

Bar

Honeycomb Stitch

Diamond

Purl Pin

Crossing of the Gimps

50 Pricking for *Ace of Clubs*

52 Technical drawing for the *Ace of Clubs*, showing a complicated movement of gimps

GROUP THREE:

Advanced

In this group of patterns you will find a selection of features and threads, and an increase in the width of the edgings. It is essential to study each pattern and locate the individual features of this lace. The reverse catchpin is very often overlooked. A new net, honeycomb stitch, will be used in several of these original designs.

Pattern 139

In this pattern you will find two familiar features: 'bars' and a 'diamond'. The 'diamond' is worked in half stitch. The honeycomb ground is introduced into this pattern. You will notice that as the edge is curved, there are small areas of cloth stitch.

Setting up
a) Start at the ft, working pin 1, hc st pin and close at pins 2–16. Work the ft at pin 17, hc st pin and close at pin 18.
b) Work the separates, in the same way at pins 19–24. Work the ft at 25 and pins 26–38.

The bar
a) Pass the LH gimp through two pairs, and the RH gimp through six pairs. With the two centre pairs work pin 39. Continue down the line working pins 40–44.
b) Pass the RH gimp through one pair to the left. Work PP 45. Pass the gimp back and work pin 46. Work the separates at pin 47 and 48. Work pin 49.
c) Pass the LH gimp through one pair to the right and work the pin at pin 50 (hc st). Pass the gimp back again and work pins 51–55. With the two centre pairs work pin 56. Pass the LH gimp to the right through five pairs.
d) Pass the RH gimp through one pair to the left. Work PP 57. Pass the RH gimp to the left through one pair. Work pin 58. Pass the RH gimp to the left through one pair, and work PP 59. Cross the gimps.
e) Return to the foot edge and work pins 60–118 (See Fig. 55).

The diamond
a) Using the pairs from pins 67 and 85, h st pin and close at pin 119. Working in numerical order, using h st, complete the diamond, finish with the two centre pairs at pin 138.
b) Work pins 139–144.

The second bar
a) Pass the LH gimp to the left through six pairs, and the RH gimp to the right through

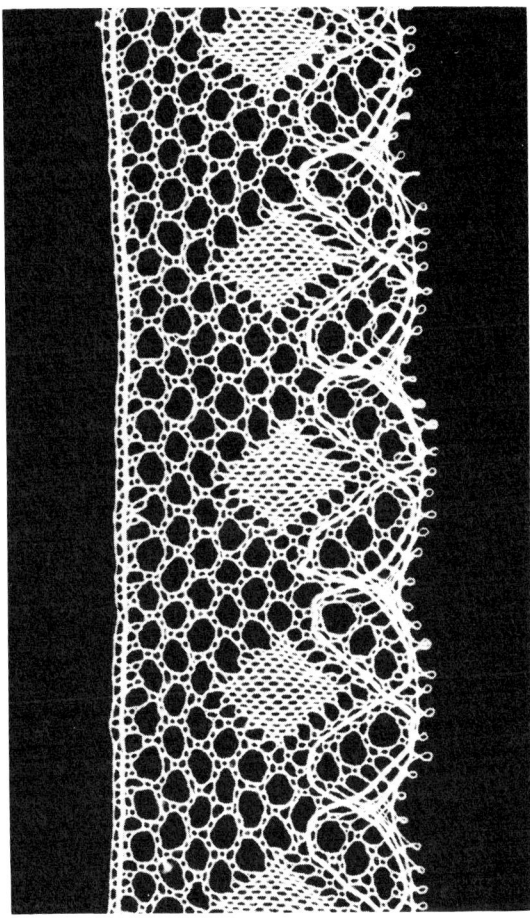

53 Pattern 139

two pairs. Twist each pair twice.
b) Work the first pin of the bar at pin 145 (hc st). At the LH side work pins 146–150. Pass the LH gimp through one pair to the right, and work pin 151 (hc st). Pass the LH gimp to the left through one pair, and work pin 152.
c) At the top of the bar, work pin 153. Pass the RH gimp to the left through one pair. Work PP 154.
d) Pass the gimp back and work the separates, pins 155 and 156. At the RH edge of the bar work pins 157–162.
e) Pass the RH gimp through six pairs to the left. Work PP 163–168. Pass the LH gimp through two pairs. Cross the gimps.

These instructions complete the heading.

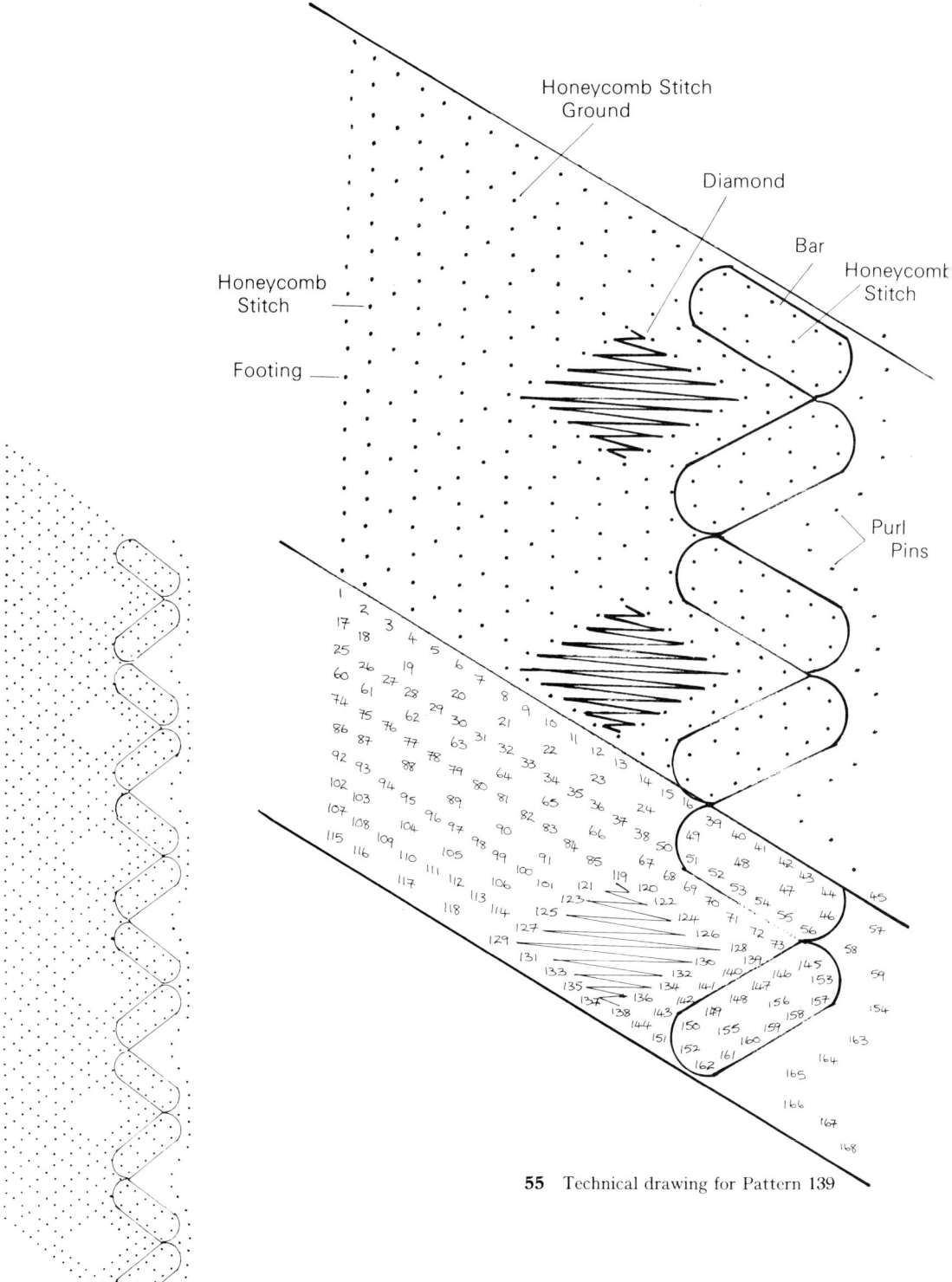

Honeycomb Stitch
Ground

Diamond

Bar

Honeycomb
Stitch

Honeycomb
Stitch

Footing

Purl
Pins

55 Technical drawing for Pattern 139

54 Pricking for Pattern 139

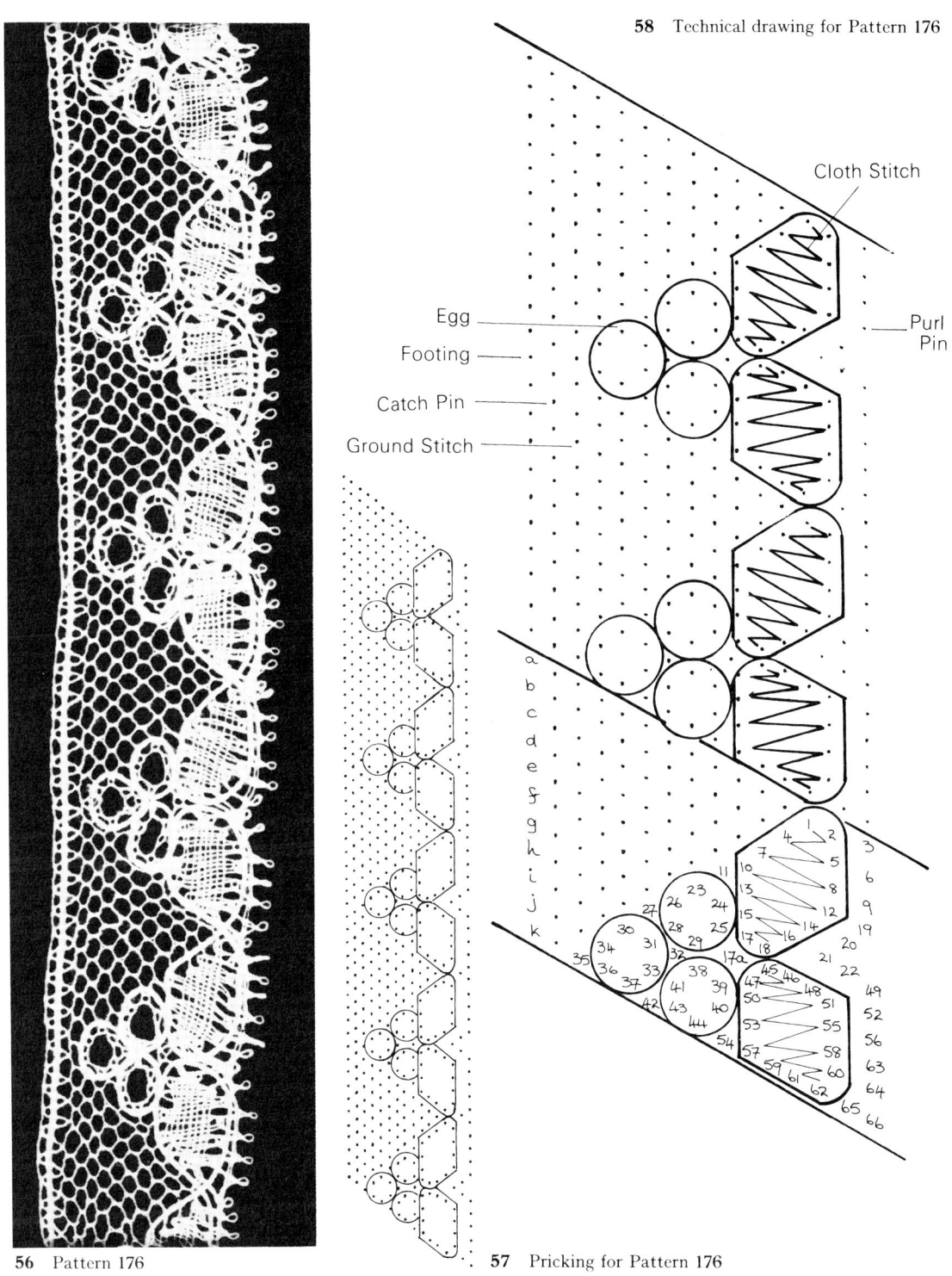

58 Technical drawing for Pattern 176

Cloth Stitch

Egg

Footing

Catch Pin

Ground Stitch

Purl
Pin

a
b
c
d
e
f
g
h
i
j
k

56 Pattern 176

57 Pricking for Pattern 176

The eggs are worked in honeycomb stitch and the leaves in cloth stitch. This pattern is worked in 120 cotton, 38 bobbins, No. 12 DMC Coton Perle, 2 gimps.

Setting up
a) Start with the ft, the cp and gr st down the line at **a** for twelve pins. Work ten more lines in the same way, **b–k**. Allow for pairs to be worked in and out of the 'eggs' and leaves.

The first leaf
a) Pass the RH gimp to the right through two pairs and the LH gimp to the left through four pairs.
b) Using the two centre pairs work a cl st, pin and close at pin 1. Cl st to the right and close the pin at pin 2.
c) Pass the RH gimp to the left through one pair. Work PP 3. Pass the RH gimp back to the right and leave.
d) Using the LH pair from pin 2, cl st to the left. Close at pin 4. Cl st to the right and close at pin 5.
e) Pass the RH gimp to the left through one pair. Work PP 6. Pass the RH gimp back. Using the worker pair from pin 5, cl st to the left. Close at pin 7.
f) Cl st to the right, close at pin 8. Work PP 9. Pass the RH gimp back to the right. Using the worker pair from pin 8, cl st across and close at pin 10.
g) Pass the LH gimp to the right through one pair and work the reverse cp at pin 11. Pass the gimp back, and using the worker from pin 10, cl st to the right. Close at pin 12. Pass the RH gimp through and work PP 19.
h) Cl st to the left and close at pin 13. A pair should be thrown out. Cl st to the right and close at pin 14. Finish this area until pin 18 is

worked. Cross the gimps. Work PP 20–22.
i) Pass the LH gimp through six pairs.

The first egg
a) Work the hc st at pins 23–25 at the RH side and pin 26 at the LH side. Pass the LH gimp to the right through one pair and work the reverse cp at pin 27.
b) Pass the gimp back and work pins 28 and 29. Pass the LH gimp to the right through two pairs and the RH gimp to the left through two pairs.
c) With the pairs from pins 17 and 25, work pin 17a. Cross the gimps.

The second egg
a) Pass the LH gimp through five pairs, and work pins 30–31. Pass the RH gimp through one pair to the left. Work a hc st at pins 32 and 33 then pass the gimp back through one pair to the right, work a hc st at pin 33. Work a hc st at pin 34. Pass the LH gimp to the right through one pair and work a reverse cp at pin 35. Pass the gimp back, and work pins 36 and 37.
b) Pass the LH gimp through five pairs. Cross the gimps. Pass each gimp through two pairs.

The third egg
a) Work pins 38–41. Pass the gimp to the right and work the reverse cp at pin 42. Pass the gimp back and work pins 43 and 44.
b) Pass the LH gimp through four pairs and cross the gimps. Pass the RH gimp through five pairs and the LH gimp through two pairs.

The second leaf
a) Work in numerical order, taking care to use the correct worker each time cl st is worked. Cross the gimps before working PP 64–66.
    These instructions complete the heading.

Pattern 181

This pattern introduces Kat Stitch. The threads already mentioned may be used, 38 bobbins, 2 gimps. Take care to follow the technical drawing when working Kat Stitch.

Setting up
a) Work the ft at pin 1, Fig. 59. Cl st to the right through two pairs. Twist the workers. Cl st and a twist with the next RH pair. Put up a

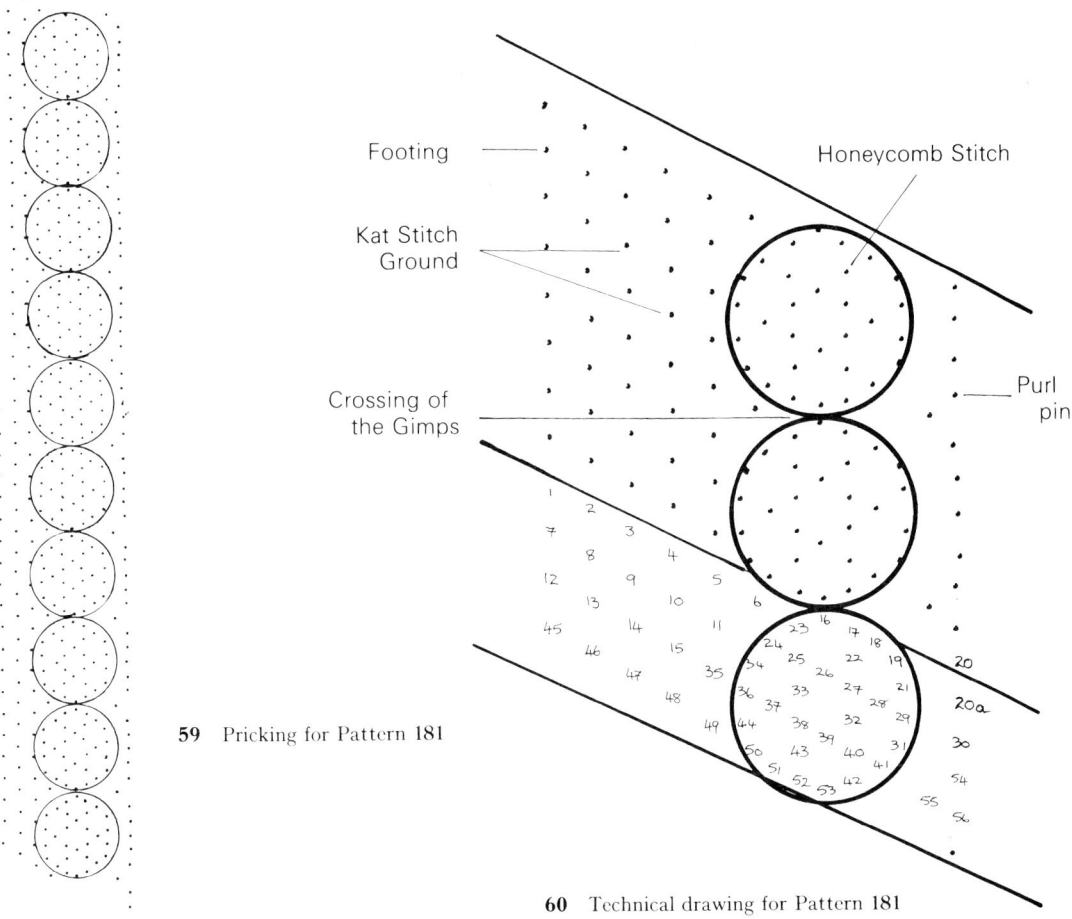

Footing

Kat Stitch
Ground

Crossing of
the Gimps

Honeycomb Stitch

Purl
pin

59 Pricking for Pattern 181

60 Technical drawing for Pattern 181

pin between the pairs at pin 2.

b) Cl st, twist each pair and repeat again. Put up a pin to the right of these pairs, pin 3.

c) Repeat at pins 4–6. Work cl st and one twist with the pairs hanging between the pins from right to left, as worked after pins 45–49. Work pins 7–15.

d) Pass the LH gimp to the left through four pairs. Pass the RH gimp to the right through four pairs.

e) With the two centre pairs work a hc st, pin and close at pin 16. Work pins 17–19 in the same way.

f) Pass the RH gimp to the left through one pair. Work PP 20.

g) Pass the RH gimp to the right and work pin 21. Work pin 22. Pass the RH gimp to the left through one pair. Work PP 20a.

h) Work pins 23–29. Pass the RH gimp to the left. Work PP 30. Return the gimp and work pin 31.

i) Work separates at pins 32 and 33. Work pin 34. Pass the LH gimp to the right through one pair and work pin 35. Cl st one twist with the pairs between pins 15 and 35.

j) Pass the LH gimp back to the left and work pins 36–42. Work separates at pin 43. Work pin 44.

k) Pass the LH gimp through one pair to the right. Work pins 45–49, in Kat Stitch. Work cl st and one twist with the pairs hanging between the pins, right to left.

l) Pass the LH gimp to the left. Work pins 50–53. Pass the LH gimp to the right through four pairs. Pass the RH gimp to the left through four pairs. Cross the gimps.

m) Work PP 54–56.

These instructions complete the heading.

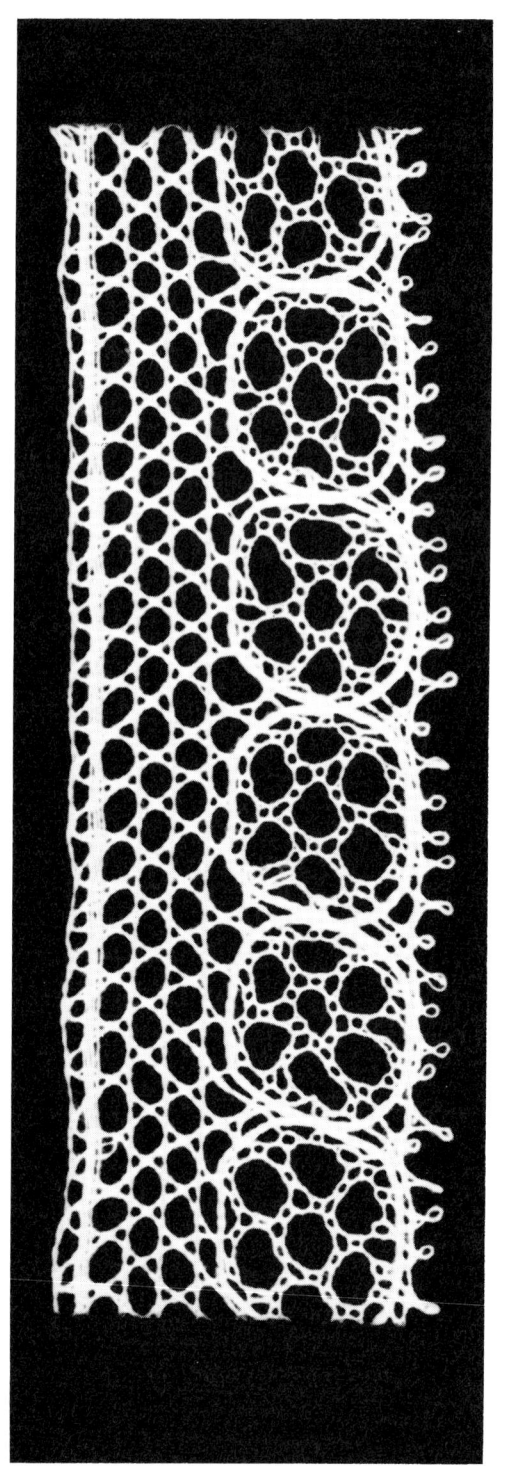

61 Pattern 181

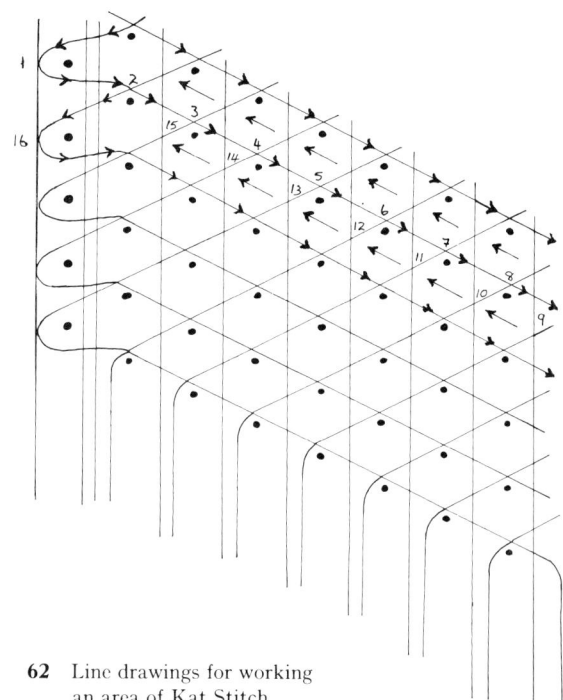

62 Line drawings for working an area of Kat Stitch

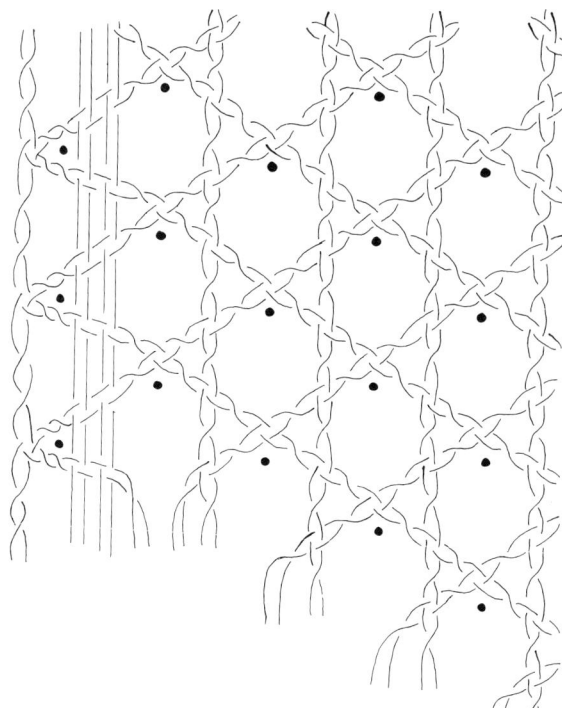

63 Details of working the footing and Kat stitch ground

The Arches

This pattern provides more practice on the hc st ground. Take care to work each second pin (at the footing) in a closed hc st pin. Use 160 cotton thread, 32 bobbins, and No. 12 DMC Coton Perle, 2 gimps.

Setting up
a)Start at the ft edge and work pin 1. Hc st, pin and close at pins 2–4. Work pins 5–14. Pass the LH gimp to the left through the pairs, from pins 4, 9, 12 and 14.

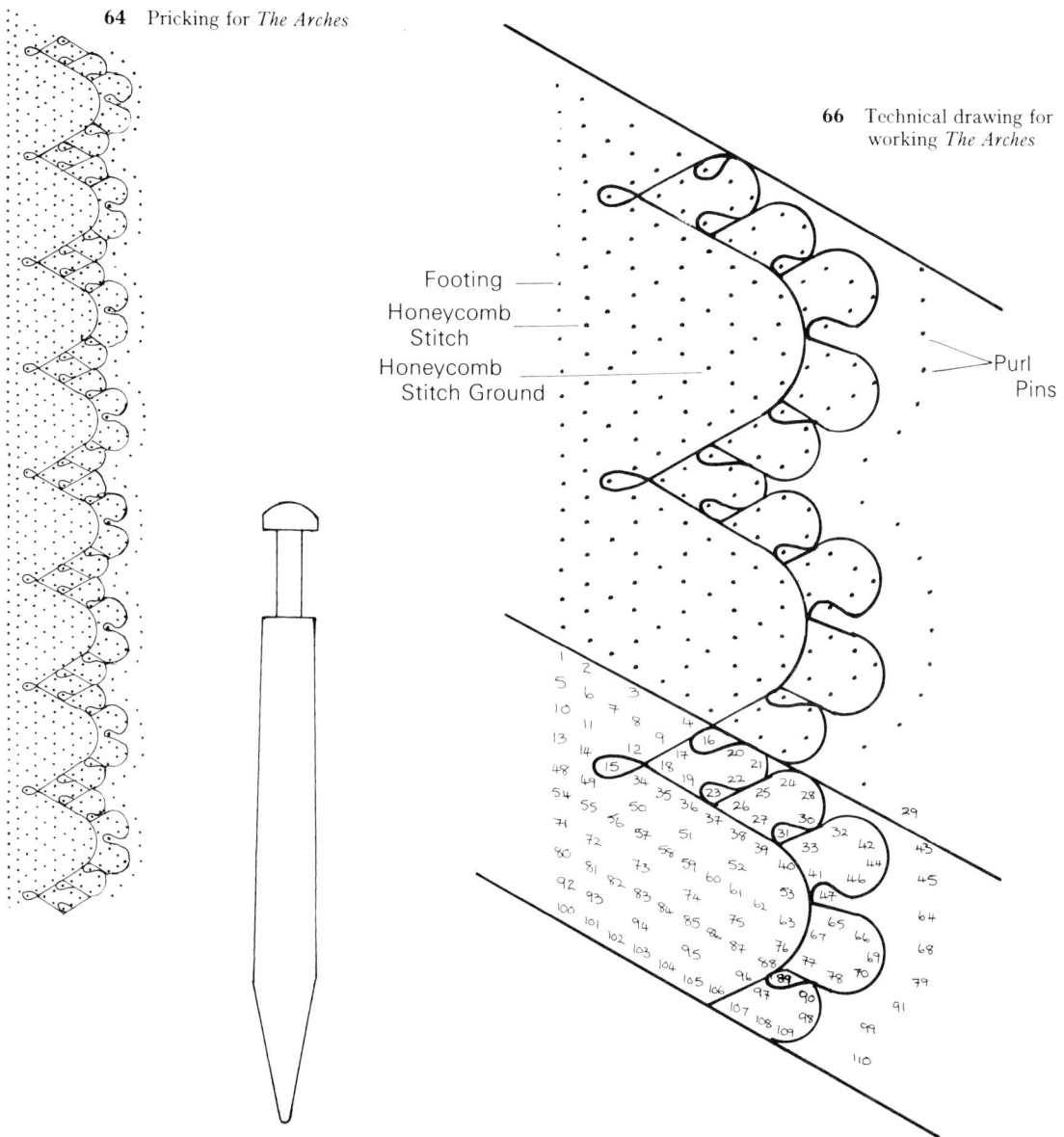

64 Pricking for *The Arches*

Footing ———
Honeycomb —
Stitch
Honeycomb —
Stitch Ground

66 Technical drawing for working *The Arches*

Purl
Pins

65 The size and shape of a Downton bobbin

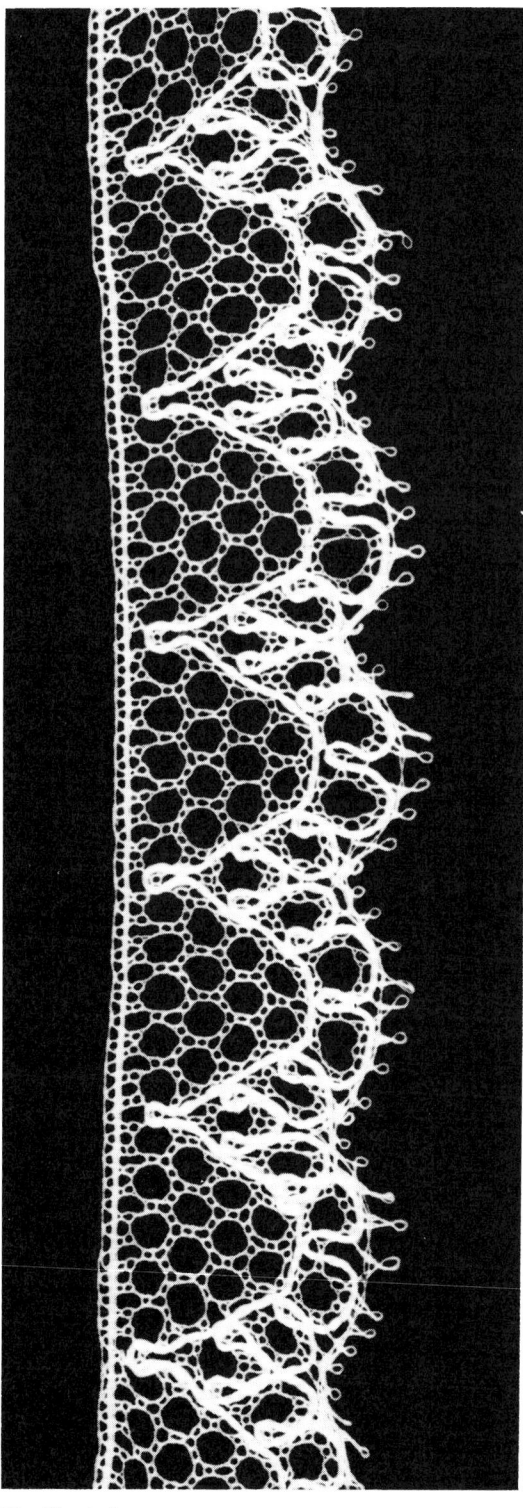

b) Work pin 15, hc st, pin and close. Work pin 16. Pass both pairs from pin 16 through the RH gimp. Work pins 17–19, hc st, pin and close. (See Fig. 66.)

c) At the RH edge, pass the RH gimp to the right through two pairs. Work pins 20–22. Pass the gimp through the pairs from pins 19 and 22. Work pin 23.

d) Pass the gimp back through the pairs from 23, 22 and 21, and a pair from the edge. Work pins 24–28. Using the RH pair from pin 28, pass the gimp to the left and work PP 29. Make sure that the correct twists are put on each pair of bobbins before and after passing the gimp threads.

e) Return to the left, pass the RH gimp to the right and work pin 30. Pass the gimp through the pair from pin 27 and the LH pair from pin 30. Work pin 31.

f) Pass the RH gimp through the pairs to the outside edge. Work pins 32 and 33.

g) Pass the LH gimp to the right, through all the pairs, and work pins 34–40.

h) Pass the LH gimp through the RH pair, from pin 40, and work pin 41.

i) Move to the outside edge, and bring the last pair of passives through the RH gimp. Remember to make one twist before passing the gimp, and two twists afterwards.

j) Work pin 42 and PP 43. Pass the RH gimp back to the right and work pin 44.

k) Pass the RH gimp to the left and work PP 45. Return the gimp and work pin 46. By moving the gimp yet again behind the pinhole, marked pin 47, work pin 47.

l) Return to the footside and work pin 48. Work pins 49–63 in the hc st ground.

m) Using the pair from pin 46, work PP 64. Pass the RH gimp through three pairs to the right, and work pins 65–67.

n) Pass the RH gimp to the left, and work PP 68. Working in numerical order, finish working the heading. Take care to pass the gimps in the correct direction, until the heading is complete.

This completes the instructions for the heading.

The Oak Leaf

Before working this pattern, study the photograph and the technical drawing carefully. There are two different shapes used in this edging. Each one contains several features of Downton Lace: the zig-zag movement of the gimp; bringing in and leaving out pairs whilst working this zig-zag edge; throwing out a pair to be used in the gr st; reverse catchpin stitches; and working the PP in advance of the rest of the lace. Work out the stages of the heading following the numbers carefully. In each 'dip' of the edge, pairs are retained for working the next heading.

120 cotton thread, 40 bobbins and No. 12 DMC Coton Perle, 2 gimps, are needed for this pattern.

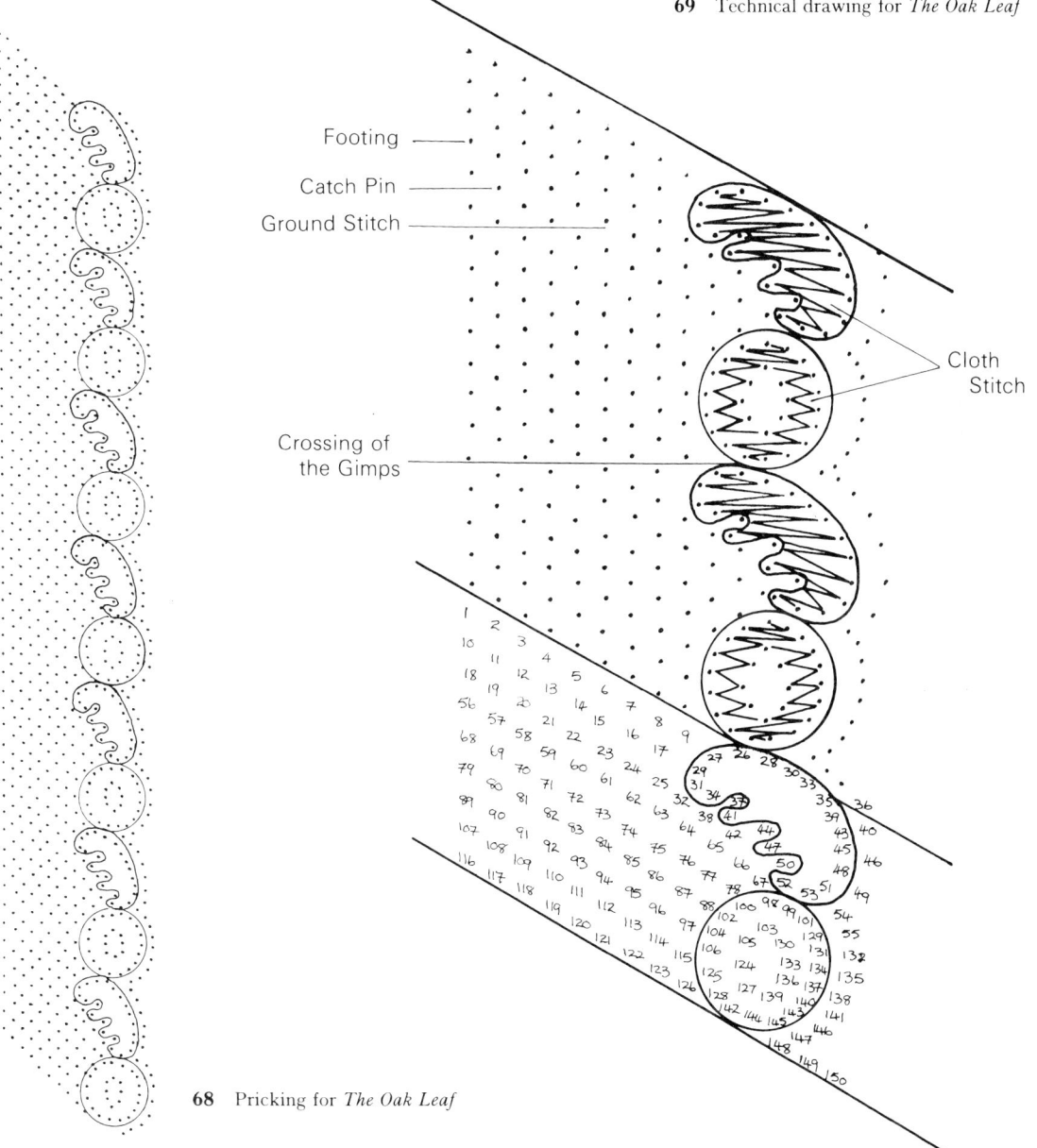

69   Technical drawing for *The Oak Leaf*

Footing

Catch Pin

Ground Stitch

Crossing of the Gimps

Cloth Stitch

68   Pricking for *The Oak Leaf*

52

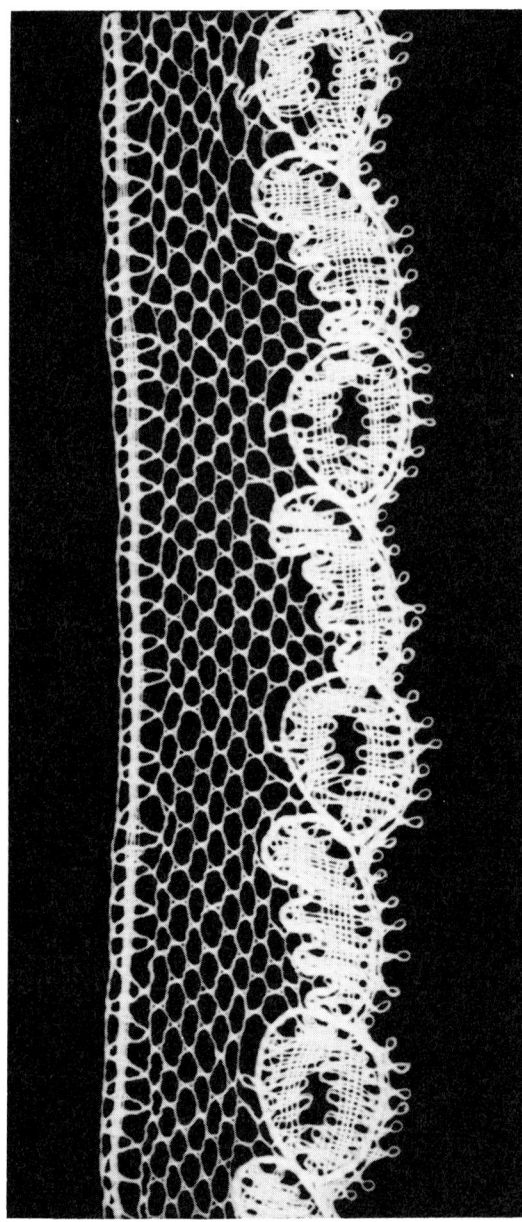

70   *The Oak Leaf*

Setting up

a) Start with the footing at pin 1, and work the area until pin 25 has been worked.

b) Pass the RH gimp to the right through three pairs and the LH gimp to the left through three pairs. Using the two centre pairs, work a cl st, pin and close pin 26. Cl st to the left and close at pin 27.

c) Cl st to the right and close at pin 28. Continue working until pin 31 has been worked. Using the pair from pin 31 pass the gimp through and work the gr st at pin 32. Pass the gimp back, cl st to the right. Close at pin 33. Work back to pin 34, pass the gimp back and leave out a pair for the zig-zag below.

d) Cl st through four more pairs, pin and close at pin 35. Work PP 36. Pass the gimp back. Using the worker pair from pin 35, cl st across towards pin 37. Work the gr st at pin 38. Pass the gimp through the worker pair. Twist the worker pair twice, and support this pair on a pin. Pass the gimp back.

e) Work across to pin 39 and close the pin. With the RH pair, pass the gimp to the left and work PP 40.

f) At this stage, make sure that the pairs thrown out at stage (c) are brought in to connect the zig-zags.

g) Work back towards pin 41. Bring in the pair previously thrown out and the gr st pair. Pin and close. Pass the gimp to the right and leave a pair out to work the gr st.

h) Work a gr st at pin 42. Work to the right and close at pin 43. Work back to the left, pass the gimp through and work pin 44 as before.

i) Work across to the right and close at pin 45. Work PP 46, pass the gimp back, and work across to close at pin 47. At this stage, look back and see that all the pairs have been taken in and left out as required.

j) Complete this section in numerical order, finishing with PP 55. Cross the gimps.

k) Look at the technical drawing, and work the foot and gr st at pins 56–67, pins 68–78, and pins 79–97, noting where the reverse catchpins are worked.

l) Work the circular area next, in numerical order. The pair used to work the PP will return as workers, joining the heading to the cl st areas.

m) At each 'dip' of the pricking, note that the PP are worked ahead of what has already been done.

n) Complete the heading in numerical order.

   This completes the instructions for the heading.

Roll and Pat of Butter

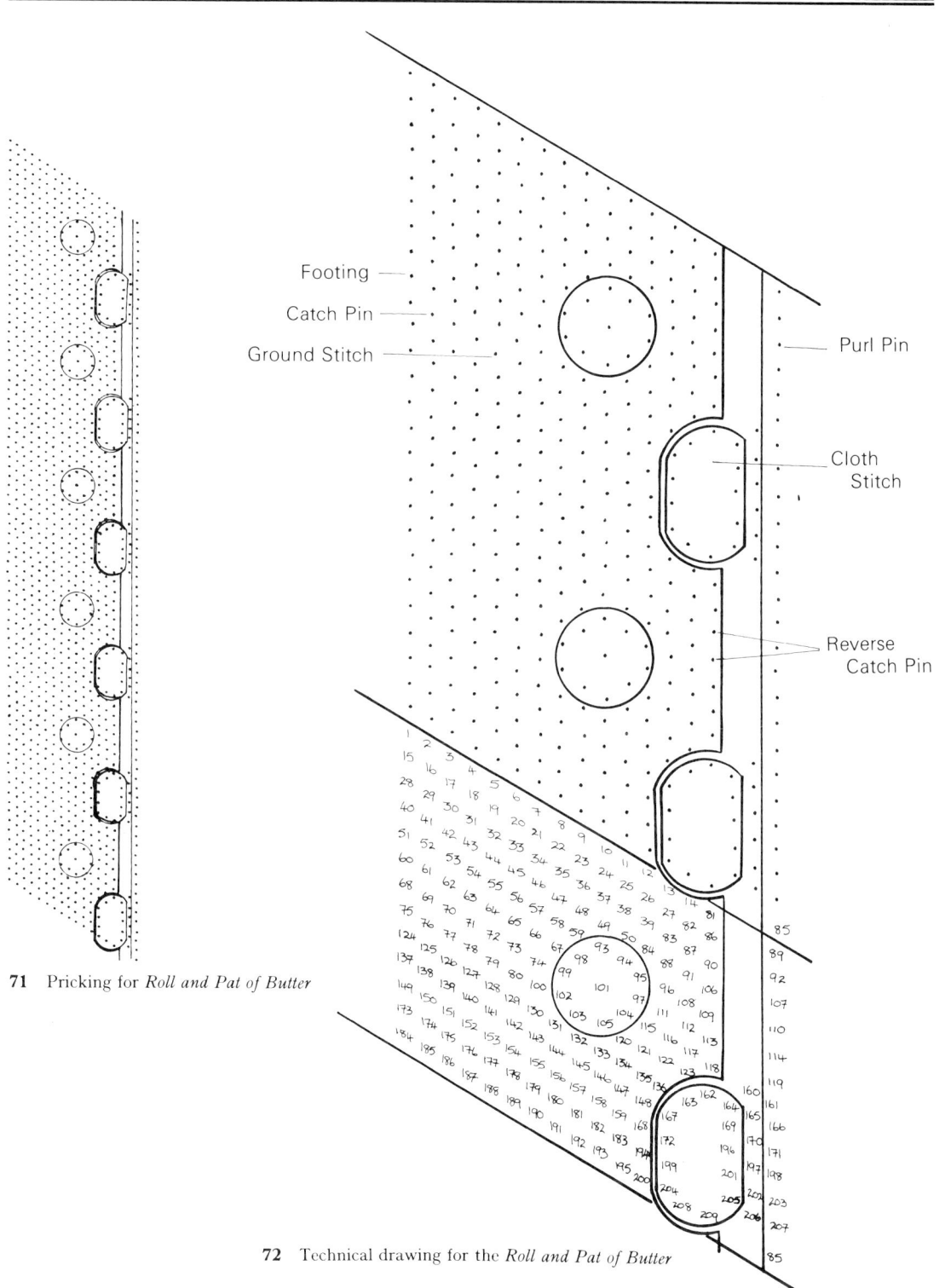

Footing

Catch Pin

Ground Stitch

Purl Pin

Cloth Stitch

Reverse Catch Pin

71 Pricking for *Roll and Pat of Butter*

72 Technical drawing for the *Roll and Pat of Butter*

This pattern is an old and traditional design. It is worked in 160 cotton thread, 42 bobbins, and No. 12 DMC Coton Perle, 4 gimps. Look at the photograph (Fig. 73) and you will see that between the 'Pat' and the edge, reverse catchpins have been used. To the left of the 'Roll', reverse catchpins are also used. A different stitch is used at the heading. There are two pairs of passive threads. This section is worked with a stitch and a twist on each pair.

Setting up
a) Work pins 1–80. Work the reverse catchpin at pin 81. Hang on a pair of gimps above pin 81 (see Fig. 72), pins 82–84, PP 85, and reverse catchpin at pin 86. Work gr st at pins 87–88.
b) Work PP 89, noting the special stitches which are worked as a PP is approached. Pass the gimp back to the right.
c) Using the pair from pin 89, work back through the gimp, and work a reverse catchpin at pin 90. Work pin 91. Work PP 92.
d) With the second pair of gimps, supported above pin 93, pass the gimp threads through five pairs above pins 93, 94, 95, 98 and 99. Twist each pair twice, and work pins 93–95 (hc st).
e) Pass the RH gimp to the left, and work a reverse catchpin at pin 96. Pass the gimp to the left, and work pin 97 (hc st).
f) Work pins 98–99, and the reverse catchpin at pin 100. Work the separates at pin 101. Work pins 102–104, and close with the centre pairs at pins 105.
g) Pass the LH gimp through six pairs, and the RH gimp through six pairs. Twist each pair three times. Lay the gimp bobbins to the rear of the work.
h) Work the reverse catchpin at pin 106, PP

107, pin 108, and reverse catchpin at 109.
i) Work the PP at 110. The pins are now worked in a new direction. Work pins 111–113, PP 114.
j) Complete the heading in numerical order, noting where the reverse catchpins are worked, and also the hc st between the 'Roll' and PP edge, at pins 160, 165, 170, 197, 202 and 206, worked to the left of the RH gimp. Pairs of gimps from the Pat are hung on above pin 162 and after pin 209 are doubled back and cut off.

This completes the instructions for the heading.

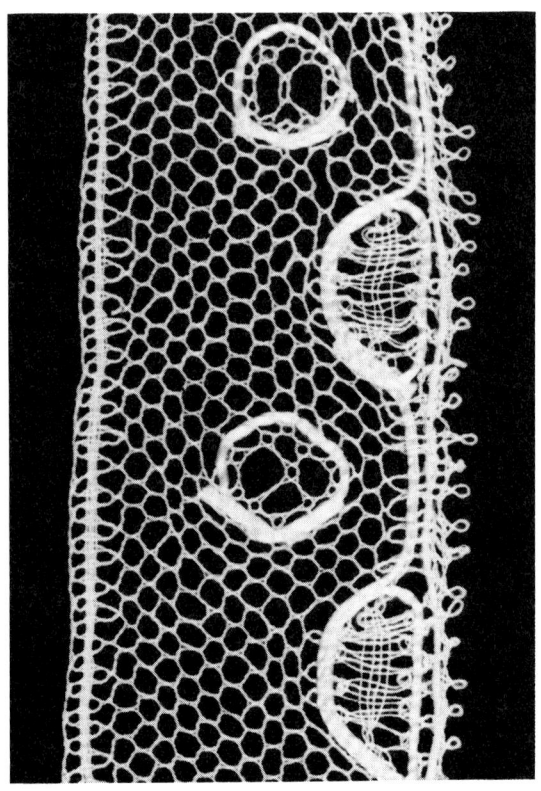

73 *Roll and Pat of Butter*

The Strawberry

By the time you reach this stage the skills of Downton lace have been practised, and with thought and application these will enable you to set up this pattern. It is a traditional pattern, requiring care and accuracy. It will be necessary to follow the technical drawing, working each section as numbered. The pattern is worked in 120 cotton, 54 bobbins, No. 12 DMC Coton Perle, 4 gimp threads.

Setting up

a) Work the footing and the ground areas, taking care to use four pairs of passive threads initially in the cl st trail at the heading. Two gimps are used in this section. There is a difference, and this must be stressed, in working the stitches at the LH and the RH side of the trail gimp threads.

b) Pass the gimp threads through the required number of pairs needed for the Strawberry.

Count the number of pairs through which the gimp thread has been passed. Work the area, using hc st ground, bringing in and throwing out pairs as and when required. Note where the gimp threads are crossed and passed close to each other so as to make a neat outline when the Strawberry is finished.

c) Make sure that all the gimp threads are worked in the correct order, passed through the correct number of pairs, and in the right direction.

74 *The Strawberry*

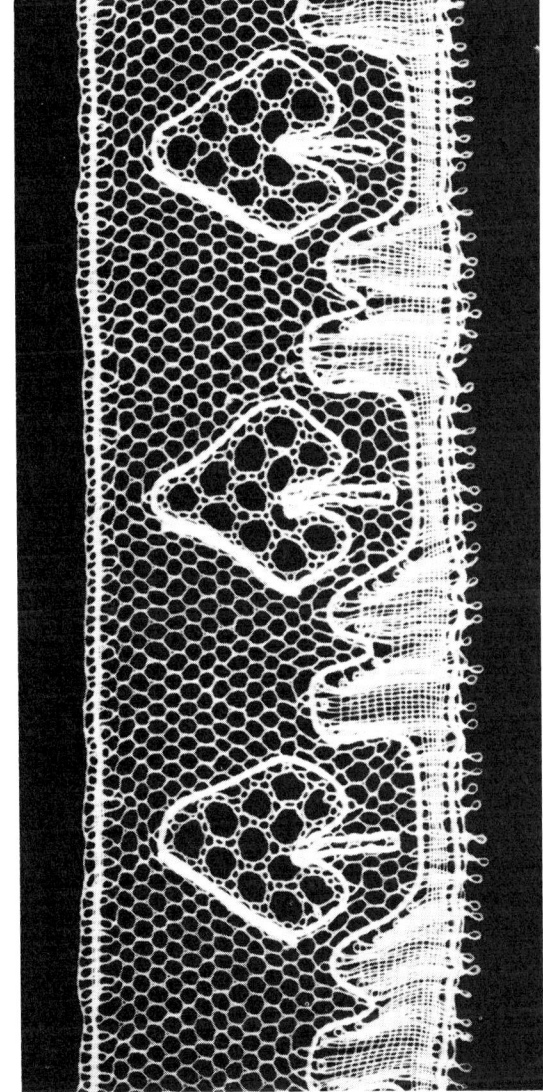

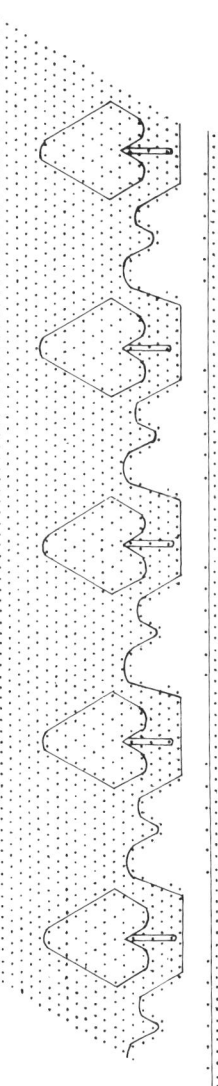

75 Pricking for *The Strawberry*

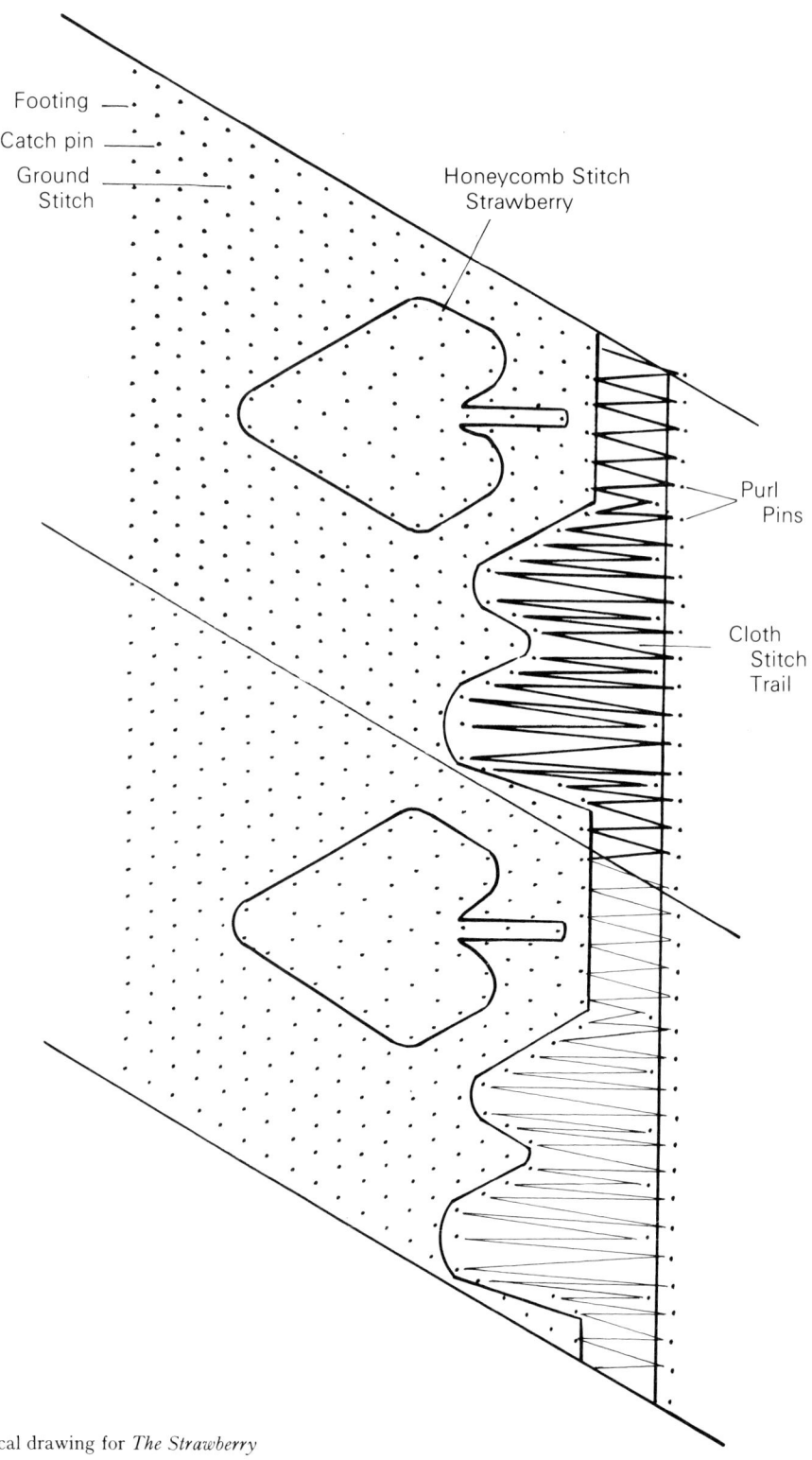

Footing
Catch pin
Ground
Stitch

Honeycomb Stitch
Strawberry

Purl
Pins

Cloth
Stitch
Trail

76 Technical drawing for *The Strawberry*

The Grecian

This pattern is an old traditional Downton lace design. A high level of skill is required to work it. 160 cotton thread, 84 bobbins, No. 12 DMC Coton Perle, 2 gimps will be needed to work this design. The technical drawing will show:

a) the footing, worked in the normal way.

b) the hc st ground.

c) the bars, the order in which they are worked, and the route in which each of the stitches are worked.

d) the h st diamonds, the order in which each is worked.

e) the gimp threads outlining the bars, and the crossing of the gimp threads.

f) the purl pins.

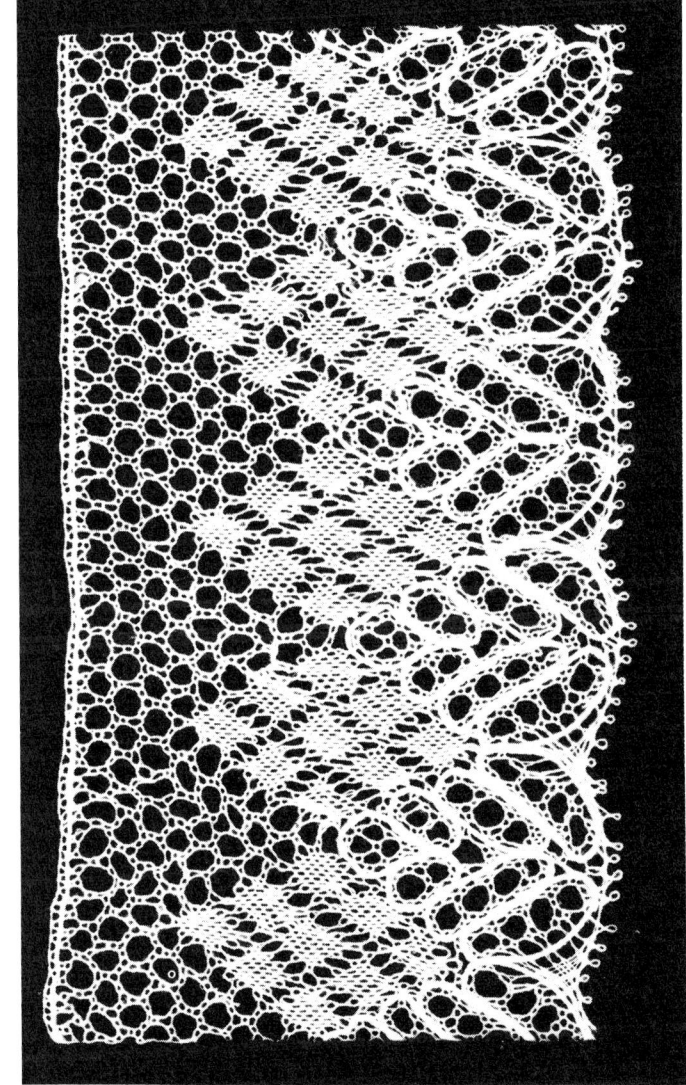

77 *The Grecian*

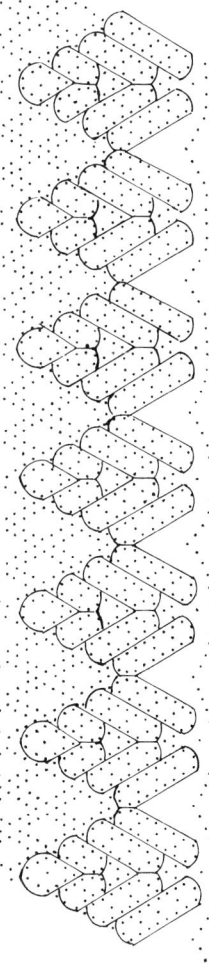

78 Pricking for *The Grecian*

58

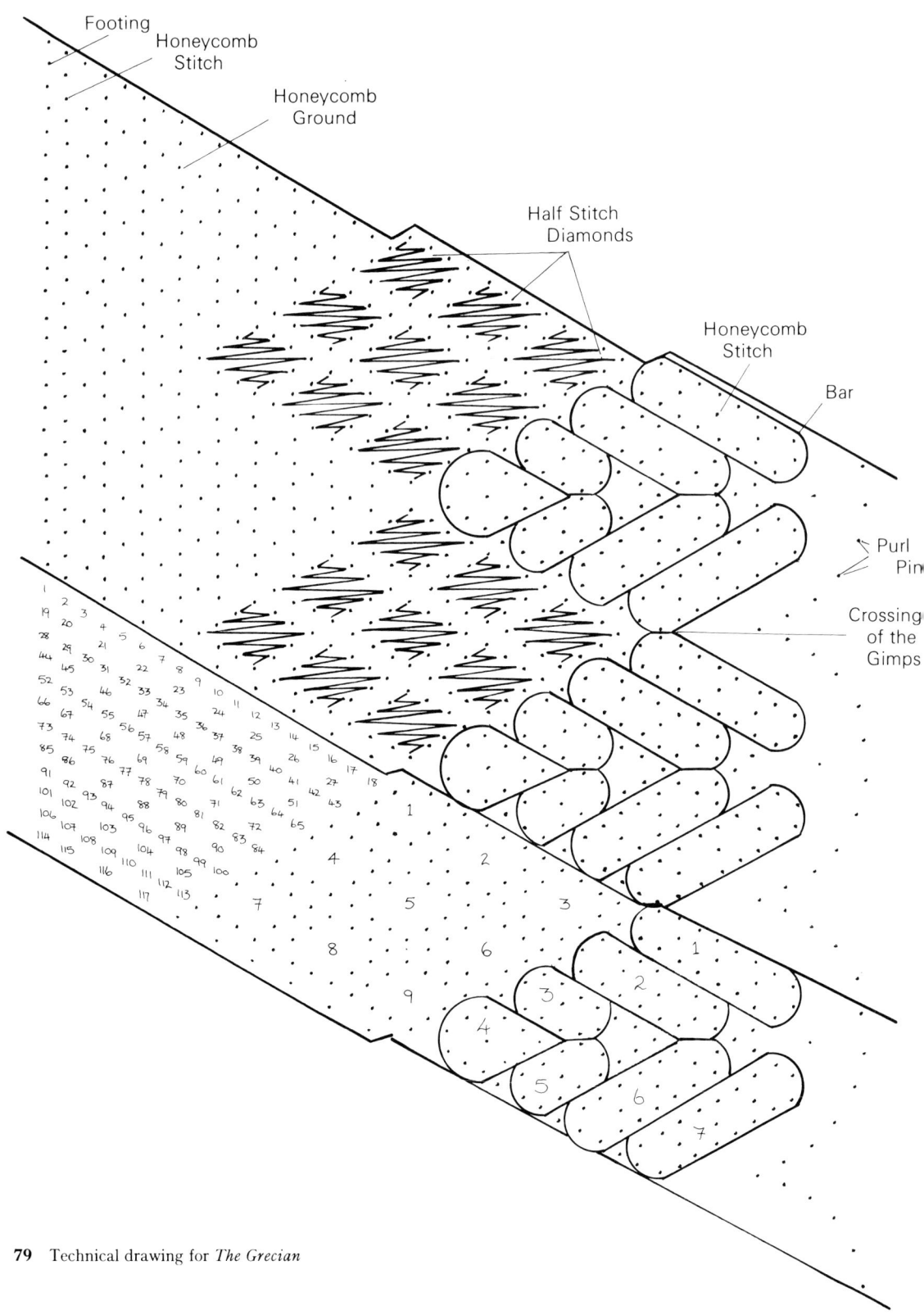

Footing
Honeycomb
Stitch
Honeycomb
Ground
Half Stitch
Diamonds
Honeycomb
Stitch
Bar
Purl
Pin
Crossing
of the
Gimps

79 Technical drawing for *The Grecian*

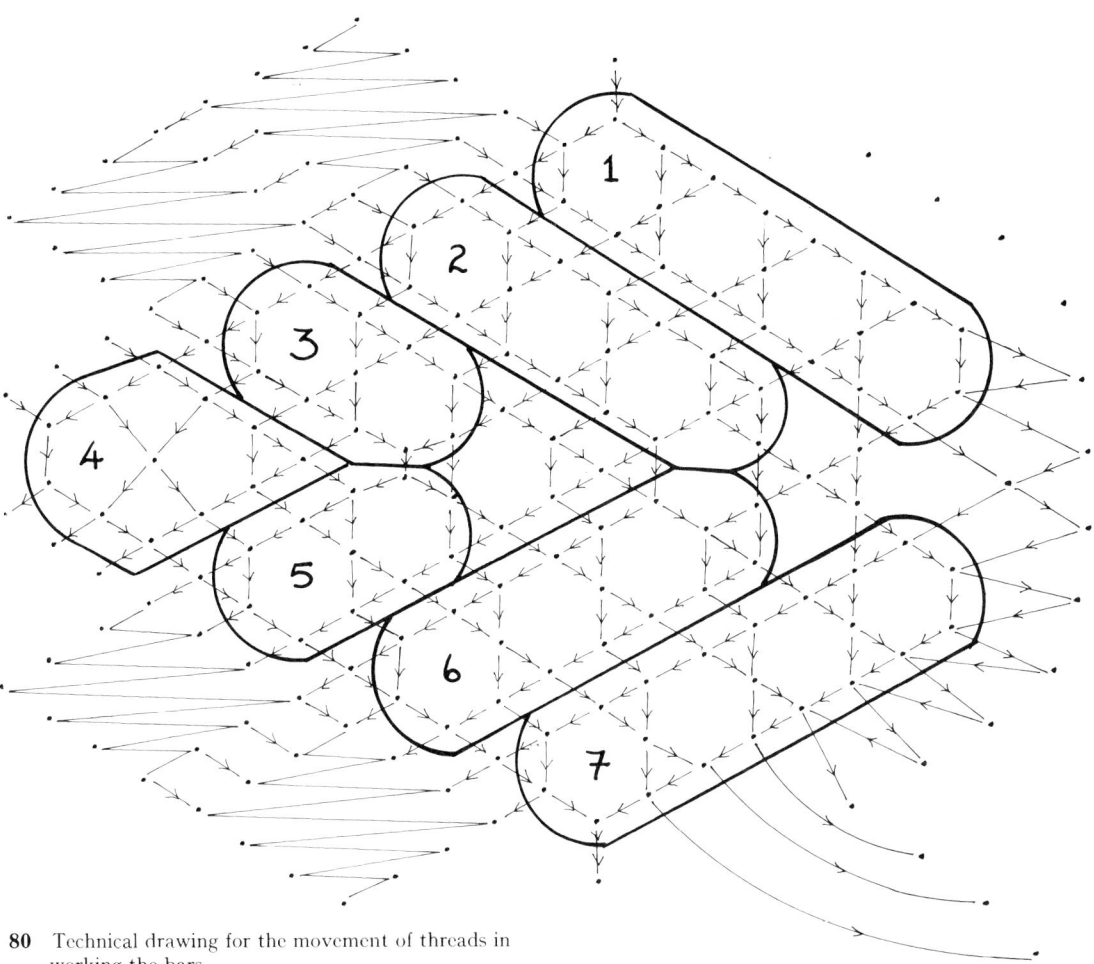

80 Technical drawing for the movement of threads in
working the bars

Pattern 59

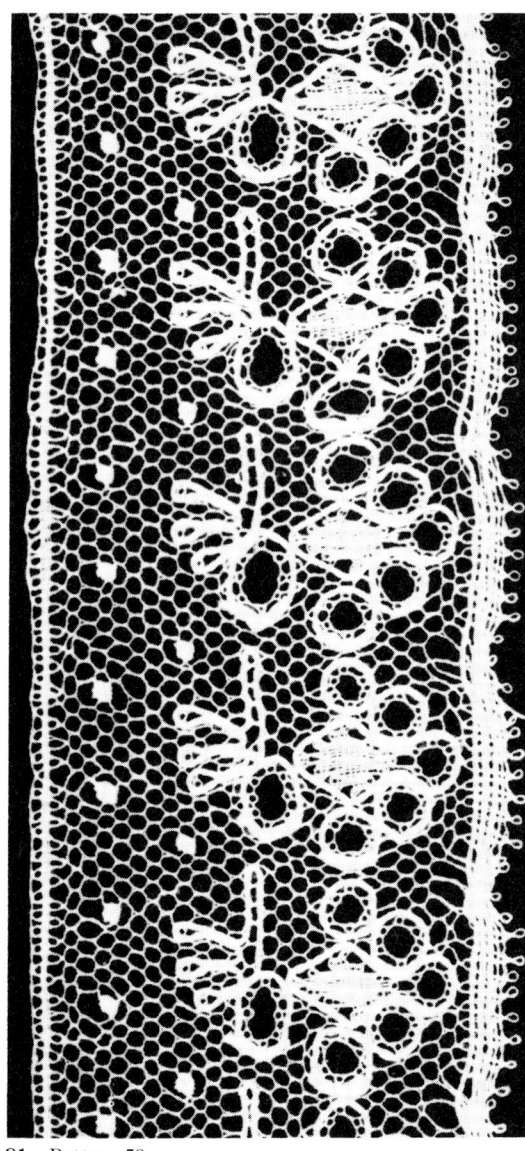

81 Pattern 59

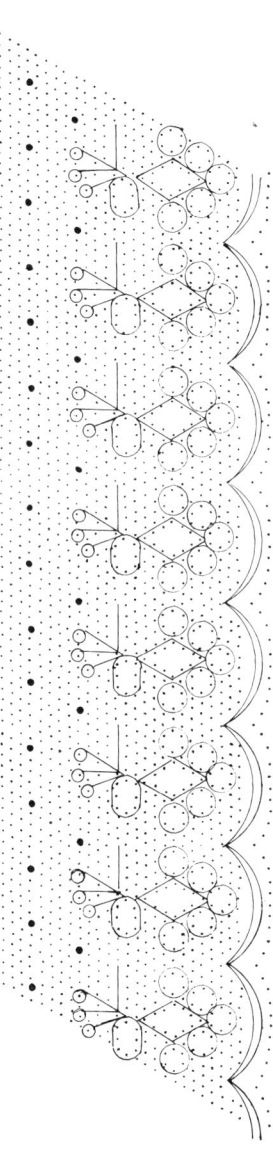

82 Pricking for Pattern 59

This pattern is worked in 160 cotton thread, 68 bobbins, and No. 12 DMC Coton Perle, 6 gimps. If you look at the technical drawing (Fig. 83) you will see that there is an alternative way of moving the gimp threads in the LH motif.

Setting up

a) Start by working the footing and the ground areas (gr st) and the tallies, ready for working the first, second, and third eggs. At the heading, the pairs between the two RH gimp threads are worked by making a cl st and a twist on each pair. Work the PP in the usual way.

b) Work the first part of the LH motif, the diamond and the fourth egg.

c) Work the footing and the gr st. Complete the LH motif, taking care to use the correct stitches. Work the last egg, the trail and PP. The area within the indentation of the curve should be neat, and the correct pairs must be taken through the gimp thread, to work the gr st above the eggs.

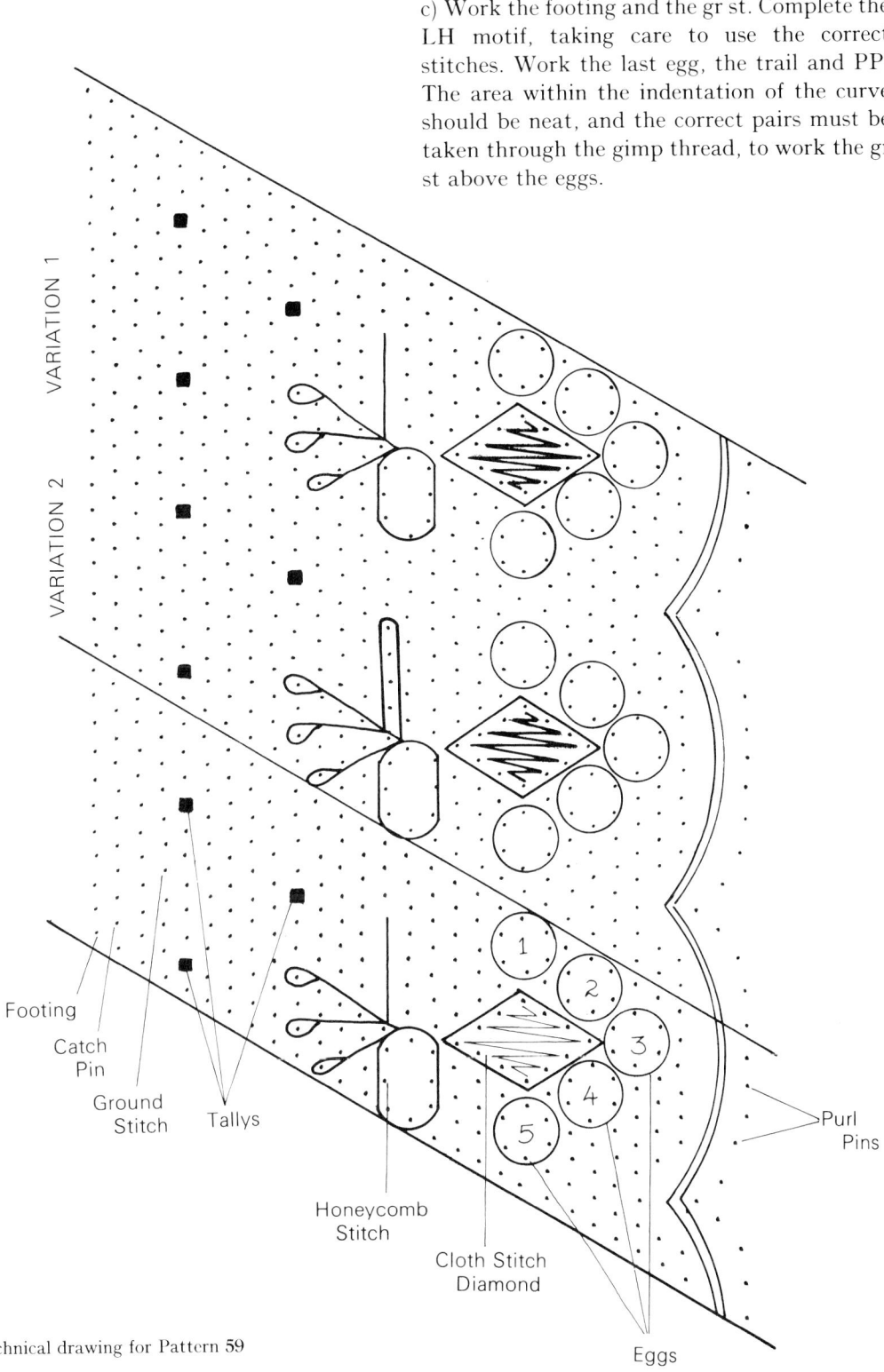

VARIATION 1

VARIATION 2

Footing

Catch
Pin

Ground
Stitch

Tallys

Honeycomb
Stitch

Cloth Stitch
Diamond

1
2
3
4
5

Purl
Pins

Eggs

83 Technical drawing for Pattern 59

SUPPLIERS

Alby Lace Centre
Cromer Road
Alby
Norwich
Norfolk

Frank Herring & Sons
27 High West Street
Dorchester
DT1 1UP

Loricraft
4 Big Lane
Lambourn
Berks
RG16 7XQ

Mace and Nairn
89 Crane Street
Salisbury
Wilts

The Lace Guild
The Hollies
53 Audnam
Stourbridge
West Midlands
DY8 4AE

D H Shaw
47 Zamor Crescent
Thurscroft
Rotherham
South Yorks

B Phillips
Pantglas
Cellen
Lampeter
Dyfed

Enid Taylor
Valley House Craft Studio
Ruston
Scarborough
North Yorks
YO13 9QE

English Lace School
Honiton Court
Rockbeare
Nr Exeter
Devon

D J Hornsby
149 High Street
Burton Latimer
Kettering
Northants

Capt J R Howell
19 Summerwood Lane
Halsall
Nr Ormskirk
Lancs
L39 8RG

Sebalace
Waterloo Mill
Howden Road
Silsden
West Yorks

John & Jennifer Ford
Upper Way
Upper Longdon
Rugeley
Staffs
WS15 1QB

Newham Lace Equipment
11 Dorchester Close
Basingstoke
Hants

George White
Delaheys Cottage
Thistle Hill
Knaresborough
North Yorks

T Brown
Woodside
Greenlands Lane
Prestwood
Great Missenden
Bucks

A Sells
49 Pedley Lane
Clifton
Shefford
Beds

C & D Springett
29 Hillmorton Road
Rugby
Warwickshire
CV22 5BE

Shireburn Lace
Finkle Court
Finkle
Sherburn in Elmet
North Yorks

Honiton Lace Shop
44 High Street
Honiton
Devon

FURTHER READING

Alice-May Bullock *Lace and Lace Making* B. T. Batsford
Eugene Close *Lacemaking* Foyles
Ann Collier *Creative Design in Bobbin Lace* B. T. Batsford
Pat Earnshaw *Bobbin and Needle Laces: Identification and Care* B. T. Batsford
Jennifer Fisher *Braid Lace for Today* Dryad Press
Mrs F. Nevill Jackson *A History of Hand-Made Lace* L. Upton Gill
Liberty & Co *Illustrated Lace Catalogue* N. D. (1908)
Valerie Paton *Creative Lace Patterns* Dryad Press
Mrs E. Bury Palliser *The History of Lace* Samson Lowe
Jean Withers *Lace to Use* Dryad Press
Jean Withers *Mounting and Using Lace* Dryad Press

INDEX

abbreviations 7
Ace of Clubs 39
Ace of Diamonds 31
Arches 49

Bar 22, 23
Bean 25

catch pin 10
Cheese Cutter 37
Church Window 22
cloth stitch 9

diamond 17, 19, 25, 29
Double Brick 20
Downton bobbin 49
Downton lace 7
Duke's Garter 24
Downton whole stitch 10

Earring 18
Egg 12
Egg and Rasher 14

foot 10
footing 12

gimp, crossing of the 13
Grecian 57
ground stitch 10

half stitch 8
honeycomb ground 43
honeycomb stitch 9

Iron 29

Kat stitch 48

Oak Leaf 51

Pattern 52 29
Pattern 53 36
Pattern 59 60
Pattern 67 34
Pattern 126 12
Pattern 139 43
Pattern 165 16
Pattern 176 45
Pattern 181 46
Pattern 186 33
purl pin 9

reverse catch pin 13
Roll and Pat of Butter 53

setting up 13
Strawberry 54

tally 35